A Beginner's Guide to Animal Cruelty and the Animal Rights Movement

Gwendolyn Buell

KNAPP BRANCH LIBRARY
13330 CONANT
DETROIT, MICHIGAN 48212
(313) 481-1772

The role of the book within our culture is changing. The change is brought on by new ways to acquire & use content, the rapid dissemination of information and real-time peer collaboration on a global scale. Despite these changes one thing is clear--"the book" in it's traditional form continues to play an important role in learning and communication. The book you are holding in your hands utilizes the unique characteristics of the Internet -- relying on web infrastructure and collaborative tools to share and use resources in keeping with the characteristics of the medium (user-created, defying control, etc.)--while maintaining all the convenience and utility of a real book.

Contents

Articles

Domestic Mistreatment of Animals — 1

- Abandoned pets — 1
- Animal hoarding — 3
- Cruelty to animals — 9

The History and Basics of Animal Testing — 19

- Animal testing — 19
- History of animal testing — 39

Animal Rights and Laws — 47

- Animal law — 47
- Animal rights — 51
- Speciesism — 77
- Animal welfare — 85
- Intrinsic value (animal ethics) — 91
- Abolitionism (animal rights) — 94
- Wildlife management — 95

Movements and Groups for Animal Rights — 100

- Veganarchism — 100
- Animal liberation movement — 105
- People for the Ethical Treatment of Animals — 115
- Animal Liberation Front — 127

References

- Article Sources and Contributors — 138

Image Sources, Licenses and Contributors

Domestic Mistreatment of Animals

Abandoned pets

Abandoned pets are pets that are, for instance, left behind when a home goes into foreclosure or their owner passes away. These animals can be left alone on the property or dropped off at a shelter. While some are left in a shelter, they are typically discovered after the foreclosure process when the realtor or bank enters the home. Realtors and banks often find these animals in poor condition due to lack of resources such as food and water. The number of abandoned pets has increased as a result of the unemployment and other economic effects of the financial crisis of 2007–2010..

Numbers of Foreclosure Pets

Currently the exact number of foreclosure pets is unknown. People often drop animals off at a shelter and claim they are moving, when in fact they are leaving due to foreclosure. However, it is expected the numbers are climbing due to high foreclosure rates. As homeowners run out of time and options, they often leave their animals behind. The animals are then classified as abandoned foreclosure pets.

Safety of Foreclosure Pets

The pets left behind in the homes are often left without food or water. Some do not survive because of the lack of resources and are found dead whenever realtors or banks enter the premises. The animals are put in harm's way, and it is often believed it is done as a way to retaliate against those who took the home away.

Pets are not able to survive in the wild without resources, which means they are at a disadvantage whenever they are left without humans to watch over them. Many are left to starve or become dehydrated.

Housing Market and Abandoned Pets

The housing market collapse has a direct impact on abandoned pets. Foreclosures went up 46% from March 2008 to March 2009, and that has caused an increase of abandoned pets. As people leave their homes, they leave their pets as well. While some do take the pets to shelters, they are still abandoning their pets because they fail to house and provide for them.

Shelters

There is currently an overcrowding at shelters which has led to 50% of all incoming animals to be euthanized. Shelters have run out of adequate space for their animals, and that has caused euthanasia rates to increase. The shelters do not have the resources to fight back against the increase in animals. Thus, pet owners that choose to drop a pet off at a shelter are only giving that pet a 50% chance of survival. However that is a bigger chance than the pet would have if he was left abandoned at home.

Adoption

While 50% of abandoned pets are euthanized, another fifty percent are adopted or end up in no kill shelters. Those that take their pet to a shelter give their pet a better chance, even though only half of pets are adopted. Unless animal shelters are able to raise more money to take care of these animals, the mortality rate will remain high. Shelters are unable to provide for the animals coming in, and they have no choice but to euthanize them. The increased number of abandoned pets has put a great deal of stress on animal shelters.

See also

- Estray

References

ASPCA (28 January 2009). "In Difficult Times, ASPCA Urges Families Facing Foreclosure: "Please, Don't Leave Your Pets Behind"" [1]. Press release. Retrieved 20 August 2009.

External links

- Click Here to Find Shelters By State [2]

Animal hoarding

Animal hoarding involves keeping higher than usual numbers of animals as pets without having the ability to properly house or care for them, while at the same time denying this inability. Compulsive hoarding can be characterized as a symptom of mental disorder rather than deliberate cruelty towards animals. Hoarders are deeply attached to their pets and find it extremely difficult to let the pets go. They typically cannot comprehend that they are harming their pets by failing to provide them with proper care. Hoarders tend to believe that they provide the right amount of care for their pets. The American Society for the Prevention of Cruelty to Animals provides a "Hoarding Prevention Team", which works with hoarders to help them attain a manageable and healthy number of pets.

Characteristics of a hoarder

An animal hoarder is distinguished from a person who keeps an unusually large number of pets, but who cares for them properly. A hoarder is distinguished from an animal breeder, who would have a large number of animals as the central component of his or her business; this distinction can be problematic, however, as some hoarders are former breeders who have ceased selling and caring for their animals, while others will claim to be breeders as a psychological defense mechanism, or in hopes of forestalling intervention. Gary Patronek defines hoarding as the "pathological human behavior that involves a compulsive need to obtain and control animals, coupled with a failure to recognize their suffering," According to another study, the distinguishing feature is that a hoarder

> "fails to provide the animals with adequate food, water, sanitation, and veterinary care, and … is in denial about this inability to provide adequate care." Along with other compulsive hoarding behaviours, it is linked in the DSM-IV to obsessive compulsive disorder and obsessive compulsive personality disorder.

Alternatively, animal hoarding could be related to addiction, dementia, or even focal delusion.

Legal solutions

United States

Many states have no legal definition for animal hoarding (though localities may have a limit of the number and types of pets), and many people are unaware of the severity of neglect in typical hoarding situations. Animals rescued from hoarders must often be cared for at the rescuer's expense, and the high cost of doing this can also act as a disincentive for prosecuting hoarding cases. These factors can make it a lengthy and challenging legal process to secure a verdict against an animal hoarder charged with animal cruelty.

In 2005, the Animal Legal Defense Fund won a significant legal victory in the Sanford, North Carolina, case *ALDF v. Woodley*. A unique North Carolina state law allows any person or organization to sue an animal abuser. In April 2005, the judge in the case granted an injunction allowing ALDF and county authorities to remove more than 300 diseased, neglected, and abused dogs from the home of a Sanford couple. ALDF was granted custody of the animals, and the hoarders were found guilty of animal cruelty charges. ALDF subsequently won the right to restrict the hoarders' visitation rights while the dogs remained in custody during ongoing appeals.

Europe

In the United Kingdom, an RSPCA spokeswoman said the society was campaigning for legislation to monitor people who took in large numbers of animals.

Dangers of hoarding animals

The health issues in animal hoarding encompass a variety of concerns related to both individual and public health. Animal hoarding is the cause of many severe health risks that threaten the hoarded animals, individuals living in hoarding residences, and surrounding neighbors.

Health effects on animals

Due to the harmful effects on the health of the animals involved, animal hoarding is considered a form of animal cruelty. Hoarders often fail to provide even basic care for their animals, and this results in disease and often death. The primary animal health issues involved are malnourishment, overcrowding, and problems related to neglect. Consequences of hoarding are long-lasting and continue to affect the animals even after they have been rescued and provided with better care.

Malnourishment

Lack of sufficient food and water is a common feature of hoarding situations. The immediate consequence of this is starvation and death. One study found at least one dead animal present in over half of the examined cases; the leading cause of death being an insufficient food and water supply. Malnourishment also leads to increased susceptibility to diseases, and the hoarded animals are often in advanced stages of sickness. Further, when there is a limited food supply, animals may resort to aggressive behavior in competing for the food, killing and sometimes even eating other animals. The hoarder's failure to provide sufficient food and water constitutes one of the principal health risks to hoarded animals.

Overcrowding

Overcrowding is also an acute animal health problem in hoarding situations. The number of animals found in hoarding cases range from dozens to several hundreds, with extreme cases reaching over a thousand. These animals are confined to houses, apartments, or even trailer-homes. In one case 306 cats were removed from a home, 87 of which were dead. Corpses were found embedded in the chimney and living room furniture. In addition to lack of living space, the extreme overcrowding facilitates the spread of diseases among animals. Furthermore, in cases where more than one species are confined to the same living spaces, the animals can pose a danger to each other due to inter-species aggression. Due to insufficient living space, the spread of disease, and close proximity to other animals, overcrowding is a major animal health concern of hoarding.

Owner neglect

Various other health problems arise from hoarders' neglect of and inability to provide basic care for the animals. Lack of veterinary attention is notable among these. Hoarders, refusing to acknowledge the deteriorating health conditions of their animals and scared they will be forced to give up custody, often refuse to bring their animals in for veterinary treatment. As a result, diseases are left untreated and allowed to become more severe. Another problem tied to neglect is poor sanitary conditions for the animals. Basic animal waste management is absent in virtually all animal-hoarding situations, and animals are found filthy and often infected with parasites as a result. Further, animals suffer behaviorally from a lack of socialization caused by an absence of normal interaction with humans and other animals. Hoarders' neglect to provide even minimal standards of care, in addition to the problems of insufficient food and severe crowding, contribute much to the health problems of animal hoarding.

Lasting consequences

Many of these health problems continue to cause suffering even after the animals are rescued. Strained animal shelters or humane societies, forced to prioritize when dealing with a large number of rescued animals, may be unable to provide immediate treatment to many animals. Further, many of the rescued animals, due to health or behavioral problems, may be un-adoptable. Euthanasia, even in cases where the animals are not beyond rehabilitation, is often the only option for rescued animals. The effects of hoarding on the health of the animals involved are severe and lasting, taking heavy tolls on both their physical and psychological well-being.

Health effects on humans

Animal hoarding also causes many health problems for the individuals involved. Hoarders, by definition, fail to correct deteriorating sanitary conditions of their living spaces, and this gives rise to several health risks for those living in and around hoarding residences. Animal hoarding is at the root of a string of human health problems including horrendous sanitation, fire hazards, zoonotic diseases, and neglect of oneself and dependents.

Sanitation concerns

Poor sanitation practices, a general characteristic of hoarding households, poses numerous health risks to inhabitants, both animal and human. In typical hoarding residences, animal waste is found coating interior surfaces, including beds, countertops, and cupboards. In one case, floors and other surfaces were found to be covered in a six-inch layer of feces and garbage.

In addition to severe odors which may pose a nuisance to neighbors, animal waste poses serious health risks in both the spread of parasites and the presence of noxious ammonia levels. OSHA, the United States agency regulating air quality standards in work-related environments, has identified an ammonia level of 300 parts per million as life-threatening for humans; in many hoarding cases the atmospheric ammonia level in the housing space approaches this number, requiring the use of protective clothing and breathing apparati during inspections or interventions. In an extreme case, the ammonia level in the hoarder's house was 152 parts per million, even after ventilation.

The presence of animal waste also prevents sanitary means of food storage and preparation, which puts residents at particular risk of contracting food-related illnesses and parasites. Insect and rodent infestation can both follow and worsen hoarding conditions, and it can potentially spread to the surrounding environment including nearby buildings. In one case, an elementary school had to be shut down due to a flea infestation that had spread from a nearby dog hoarder residence.

Hoarders are frequently found to collect large numbers of inanimate objects in addition to animals, giving rise to extreme clutter as well. Hoarded objects can include newspapers, trash, clothing, and food; and the clutter inhibits normal movement around the house, hampering household maintenance and sanitary food preparation; heightening risks of accidents and contributing to the overall level of squalor. A lack of functioning utilities, such as toilets, sinks, electricity, or proper heating (often for non-payment of bills, a common theme in cluttering, though poor maintenance may also be a cause) further exacerbates the problem. Fire hazards comprise yet another health issue tied to poor sanitation; the clutter found in many hoarding households prevents workable fire escape plans and serves as a possible fuel when located close to heat sources. The risk is amplified when hoarders, due to inoperative normal heating systems, seek alternate heating methods such as fire places, stoves, or kerosene heaters.

Zoonotic diseases

Another human health issue caused by animal hoarding is the risk of zoonotic diseases. Defined as "human diseases acquired from or transmitted to any other vertebrate animal," zoonotic diseases can often be lethal and in all cases constitute a serious public health concern. Examples of well-known zoonotic diseases include bubonic plague, influenza, and rabies. Common domesticated animals constitute a large portion of animals carrying zoonoses, and as a result, humans involved in animal hoarding situations are at particular risk of contracting disease. Zoonoses that may arise in hoarding situations—through means such as dog, cat, or rat bites—include rabies, salmonellosis, catscratch fever, hookworm, and ringworm. One zoonosis of special concern is toxoplasmosis, which can be transmitted to humans through cat feces or badly prepared meat, and is known to cause severe birth defects or stillbirth in the case of infected pregnant women. The risk of zoonotic diseases is amplified by the possibility of community epidemics. Overall, zoonotic diseases constitute a major human health issue related to animal hoarding.

Self-neglect and child/elder abuse

Main article: Diogenes syndrome

The problems of self-neglect and elder and child abuse are also health problems associated with animal hoarding. Self-neglect can be defined as "the inability to provide for oneself the goods or services to meet basic needs," and has been shown to be an "independent risk factor for death". While self-neglect is a condition generally associated with the elderly, animal hoarders of any age can and do suffer from it. This is demonstrated by the fact that hoarders' lifestyles often match the degenerate sanitary conditions that surround them. Child and elder abuse arise when dependents are living with the hoarder. According to one study, dependents lived with the hoarder in over half of the cases. As with his or her animals, the hoarder often fails to provide adequate care for dependents both young and old, who suffer from a lack of basic necessities as well as the health problems caused by unsanitary conditions. In one case, two children of a couple hoarding 58 cats and other animals were forced to repeat kindergarten and first grade because of excessive absence due to respiratory infections. Self-neglect and neglect of dependents make up a major human health concern of animal hoarding.

Mental health issues

Though it has not been firmly linked to any specific psychological disorder, evidence suggests that there is "a strong mental health component" in animal hoarding. Models that have been projected to explain animal hoarding include delusional disorder, attachment disorder, obsessive–compulsive disorder, zoophilia, dementia, and addiction. Direct evidence for most is lacking, however.

Delusional Disorder

Animal hoarders display symptoms of delusional disorder in that they have a "belief system out of touch with reality". Virtually all hoarders lack insight into the extent of deterioration in their habitations and on the health of their animals, refusing to acknowledge that anything is wrong. Further, hoarders may believe they have "a special ability to communicate and/or empathize with animals," rejecting any offers of assistance. Delusional disorder is an effective model in that it offers an explanation of hoarder's apparent blindness to the realities of their situations.

Attachment Disorder

Another model that has been suggested to explain animal hoarding is attachment disorder, which is primarily caused by poor parent-child relationships during childhood. It is characterized by an inability to form "close relationships [with other humans] in adulthood". As a result, those suffering from attachment disorder may turn to animals for companionship. Interviews with animal hoarders have revealed that hoarders have often experienced domestic trauma in childhood, which is the basis of the evidence for this model.

Obsessive–compulsive Disorder

Perhaps the strongest psychological model put forward to explain animal hoarding is obsessive–compulsive disorder (OCD). An overwhelming sense of responsibility for something is characteristic of OCD patients, who then take unrealistic measures to fulfill their perceived duty. Animal hoarders often feel a strong sense of responsibility to take care of and protect animals, and their solution—that of acquiring as many animals as they possibly can—is clearly unrealistic. Further, the hoarding of inanimate objects, practiced by a majority of animal hoarders, is a fairly common occurrence in OCD patients. These connections between animal hoarding and obsessive–compulsive disorder suggest that OCD may be a useful model in explaining animal hoarding behavior.

In popular culture and fiction

- On Animal Planet's Confessions: Animal Hoarding [1], friends and family of animal hoarders intervene to offer them support to make a change [2] in the form of psychological help and veterinary care or placement for their pets.
- In the animated series *The Simpsons* animal hoarding is represented by the semi-recurring character Crazy Cat Lady, whose real name is Eleanor Abernathy. She is a mentally ill old woman covered by cats who is often seen speaking in gibberish and throwing cats at people.

See also

- Cat lady
- Geriatric medicine
- Monomania

External links

- Confessions: Animal Hoarding [1] on Animal Planet
- Animal Hoarding documentary project [3]
- Inside Animal Hoarding (with video) [4]
- People Who Hoard Animals [5], *Psychiatric Times*

- Behind Closed Doors: The Horrors of Animal Hoarding [6], Humane Society of the United States
- The Hoarding of Animals Research Consortium [7], Tufts University
- Animal Hoarding [8], American Society for the Prevention of Cruelty to Animals
- Animal Legal Defense Fund [9]
- Animal Hoarding: Alone in a Crowded Room [10]
- News and information on animal hoarding and large scale animal cruelty [11]

Cruelty to animals

Cruelty to animals is the infliction of suffering or harm upon animals, other than humans, for purposes other than self-defense. More narrowly, it can be harm for specific gain, such as killing animals for food or for their fur. Diverging viewpoints are held by jurisdictions throughout the world.

Broadly speaking, there are two approaches to the issue. The animal welfare position holds that there is nothing inherently wrong with using animals for human purposes, such as food, clothing, entertainment, and research, but that it should be done in a humane way that minimizes unnecessary pain and suffering. Animal rights theorists criticize this position, arguing that the words "unnecessary" and "humane" are subject to widely differing interpretations, and that the only way to ensure protection for animals is to end their status as property, and to ensure that they are never used as commodities. Laws concerning animal cruelty are designed to prevent needless cruelty to animals, rather than killing for other aims such as food, or they concern species not eaten as food in the country involved, such as those regarded as pets.

In law

Many jurisdictions around the world have enacted statutes which forbid cruelty to some animals but these vary by country and in some cases by the use or practice.

Australia

In Australia, many states have enacted legislation outlawing cruelty to animals, however, it is argued that welfare laws do not adequately extend to production animals. Whilst police maintain an overall jurisdiction in prosecution of criminal matters, in many states officers of the RSPCA and other animal welfare charities are accorded authority to investigate and prosecute animal cruelty offenses.

China

As of 2006 there were no laws in China governing acts of cruelty to animals. In certain jurisdictions such as Fuzhou, dog control officers may kill any unaccompanied dogs on sight. However, the People's Republic of China is currently in the process of making changes to its stray-dog population laws in the capital city, Beijing. Mr. Zheng Gang who is the director of the Internal and Judicial Committee which comes under the Beijing Municipal People's Congress (BMPC), supports the new draft of the Beijing Municipal Regulation on Dogs from the local government. This new law is due to replace the current Beijing Municipal Regulation on Dog Ownership, introduced in 1889. The current regulation talks of "strictly" limiting dog ownership and controlling the number of dogs in the city. The new draft focuses instead on "strict management and combining restrictions with management." There are no government supported charitable organizations like the RSPCA, which monitors the cases on animal cruelty, so that all kinds of animal abuses, such as to fish, tigers, and bears, are to be reported for law enforcement and animal welfare.

In September 2009, legislation was drafted to address deliberate cruelty to animals in China. If passed, the legislation would offer some protection to pets, captive wildlife and animals used in laboratories, as well as regulating how farm animals are raised, transported and slaughtered.

Hong Kong

Hong Kong has a law titled "Prevention of Cruelty to Animals Regulations", with a maximum 3 year imprisonment and fines of HKD$200,000.[citation needed]

Japan

Animal experiments are regulated by the 2000 Law for the Humane Treatment and Management of Animals, which was amended in 2006. This law requires those using animals to follow the principles outlined in the 3Rs and use as few animals as possible, and cause minimal distress and suffering. Regulation is at a local level based on national guidelines, but there are no governmental inspections of institutions and no reporting requirement for the numbers of animals used.

Egypt

Egyptian law states that anyone who inhumanely beats or intentionally kills any domesticated animal may be jailed or fined, however, these laws are rarely enforced. The Egyptian Society for the Prevention of Cruelty to Animals was established by the British over a hundred years ago, and is currently administered by the Egyptians. The SPCA was instrumental in promoting a 1997 ban on bullfighting in Egypt.

In the ancient Egyptian law, the killers of cats or dogs were executed.

Saudi Arabia

Despite passages in the Qur'an advocating positive treatment of animals, veterinarian Lana Dunn and several Saudi nationals report that there are no laws to protect animals from cruelty since the term is not well-defined within the Saudi legal system. They point to a lack of a governing body to supervise conditions for animals, particularly in pet stores and in the exotic animal trade with East Africa.

Taiwan

The Taiwanese Animal Protection Law was passed in 1998, imposing fines for cruelty. Criminal penalties for animal cruelty were enacted in 2007, including a maximum of 1 year imprisonment.[citation needed]

Europe

Germany, Switzerland, Sweden, and Austria have all banned battery cages for egg-laying hens. The entire European Union is phasing out battery cages by 2012.

Germany

In Germany, killing animals or causing significant pain (or prolonged or repeated pain) to them is punishable by imprisonment of up to three years or a financial penalty. If the animal is of foreign origin, the act may also be punishable as criminal damage.

Italy

Acts of cruelty against animals can be punished with imprisonment, for a minimum of three months up to a maximum of three years, and with a fine ranging from a minimum of 3000 Euros to a maximum of 160,000 Euros, as for the law n°189/2004[citation needed]. The law was passed mainly to crush the phenomenon of dog fighting, which in Italy is a clandestine blood sport fully controlled by organized crime.

United Kingdom

In the United Kingdom, cruelty to animals is a criminal offence for which one may be jailed for up to 51 weeks and may be fined up to £20,000.

On August 18, 1911, the House of Commons introduced the Protection of Animals Act 1911 (c.27) following lobbying by the Royal Society for the Prevention of Cruelty to Animals (RSPCA). The maximum punishment was 6 months of "hard labour" with a fine of 25 pounds.

Switzerland

The Swiss animal protection laws are among the strictest in the world, comprehensively regulating the treatment of animals including the size of rabbit cages, and the amount of exercise that must be provided to dogs.

In the canton of Zurich an animal lawyer, Antoine Goetschel, is employed by the canton government to represent the interests of animals in animal cruelty cases.

Mexico

In Mexico, there are little to no animal cruelty laws, however, it has been suggested that animal cruelty laws are slowly being implemented. The country's current policy usually condemns physical harm to animals as property damage to the owners of the abused animal. The Law of Animal Protection of the Federal District is wide-ranging, based on banning 'unnecessary suffering'. Similar laws now exist in most states. However, this is disregarded by much of the public and authorities.

United States

The primary federal law relating to animal care and conditions in the US is the Animal Welfare Act of 1966, amended in 1970, 1976, 1985, 1990, 2002 and 2007. It is the only Federal law in the United States that regulates the treatment of animals in research, exhibition, transport, and by dealers. Other laws, policies, and guidelines may include additional species coverage or specifications for animal care and use, but all refer to the Animal Welfare Act as the minimum acceptable standard.

The AWA has been criticized by animal rights groups for excluding birds, rats and mice bred for research, as well as animals intended to be used for food or fiber; as well as all cold-blooded animals.

The Animal Legal Defense Fund releases an annual report ranking the animal protection laws of every state based on their relative strength and general comprehensiveness. In 2008's report, the top five states for their strong anti-cruelty laws were California, Illinois, Maine, Michigan, and Oregon. The five states with the weakest animal cruelty laws were Arkansas, Idaho, Kentucky, Mississippi, and North Dakota.

In Massachusetts and New York, agents of humane societies and associations may be appointed as special officers to enforce statutes outlawing animal cruelty.

In 2004, a Florida legislator proposed a ban on "cruelty to bovines," stating: "A person who, for the purpose of practice, entertainment, or sport, intentionally fells, trips, or otherwise causes a cow to fall or lose its balance by means of roping, lassoing, dragging, or otherwise touching the tail of the cow commits a misdemeanor of the first degree." The proposal did not become law.

In the United States, ear cropping, tail docking, the Geier Hitch, rodeo sports, and other acts are sometimes condoned. Penalties for cruelty can be minimal, if pursued. Currently, 46 of the 50 states have enacted felony penalties for certain forms of animal abuse. However, in most jurisdictions, animal cruelty is most commonly charged as a misdemeanor offense. In one recent California case, a felony conviction for animal cruelty could theoretically net a 25 year to life sentence due to their three-strikes law, which increases sentences based on prior felony convictions.

In 2003, West Hollywood, California passed an ordinance banning declawing of house cats. In 2007, Norfolk, Virginia passed legislation only allowing the procedure for medical reasons. However, most jurisdictions allow the procedure. It is illegal in many parts of Europe.

Welfare laws

Several states have enacted or considered laws in support of humane farming.

- On November 5, 2002, Florida voters passed Amendment 10 by a margin of 55% for, amending the Florida Constitution to ban the confinement of pregnant pigs in gestation crates.
- On January 14, 2004, the bill AB-732 died in the California Assembly's Agriculture Committee. The bill would have banned gestation and veal crates, eventually being amended to include only veal crates. On May 9, 2007, the bill AB-594 was withdrawn from the California State Assembly. The bill had been effectively killed in the Assembly Agriculture Committee, by replacing the contents of the bill with language concerning tobacco cessation coverage under Medi-Cal. AB-594 was very similar to the current language of Proposition 2.
- On November 7, 2006, Arizona voters passed Proposition 204 with 62% support. The measure prohibits the confinement of calves in veal crates and breeding sows in gestation crates.[citation needed]
- On June 28, 2007, Oregon Governor Ted Kulongoski signed a measure into law prohibiting the confinement of pigs in gestation crates (SB 694, 74th Leg. Assembly, Regular Session).
- In January 2008, Nebraska State Senate bill LB 1148, to ban the use of gestation crates for pig farmers, was withdrawn within 5 days amidst controversy.
- On May 14, 2008, Colorado Governor Bill Ritter signed into law a bill, SB 201, that phases out gestation crates and veal crates.

Canada

The Animal Legal Defense Fund releases an annual report ranking the animal protection laws of every province and territory based on their relative strength and general comprehensiveness. In 2009's report, the top four, for their strong anti-cruelty laws, were British Columbia, Manitoba, Nova Scotia, and Ontario. The worst four were New Brunswick, Northwest Territories, Nunavut, and Quebec.

In theory and practice

There are many reasons why individuals abuse animals. Animal cruelty covers a wide range of actions (or lack of action). Learning about animal abuse has revealed patterns of behavior employed by abusers.

Animal cruelty is often broken down into two main categories: active and passive, also referred to as commission and omission, respectively.

Passive cruelty is typified by cases of neglect, in which the cruelty is a lack of action rather than the action itself. Examples of neglect are starvation, dehydration, parasite infestations, allowing a collar to grow into an animal's skin, inadequate shelter in extreme weather conditions, and failure to seek veterinary care when necessary.

In many cases of neglect in which an investigator believes that the cruelty occurred out of ignorance, the investigator may attempt to educate the pet owner, then revisit the situation. In more severe cases, exigent circumstances may require that the animal be removed for veterinary care.

Active cruelty implies malicious intent, as when a person has deliberately and intentionally caused harm to an animal, and is sometimes referred to as NAI (Non-Accidental Injury). Acts of intentional animal cruelty may be indicators of serious psychological problems. There is an intrinsic link between battered pets and battered women and children. The likelihood that women's shelter personnel will encounter women and children who have been threatened by batterers using animal abuse as a weapon is high. This is because more families in America have pets than have children. Secondly, the majority of pet owners are themselves parents with children. Thirdly, 64.1% of households with children under age 6, and 74.8% of households with children over age 6, also have pets. Lastly, as many as 71% of pet-owning women seeking shelter at safe houses have reported that their partner had threatened and/or actually hurt or killed one or more of their pets; 32% of these women reported that one or more of their children had also hurt or killed pets. Battered women report that they are prevented from leaving their abusers because they fear what will happen to the animals in their absence. Animal abuse sometimes is used as a form of intimidation in domestic disputes.

Medicine

Animal testing, Traditional medicine

Psychological disorders

One of the known warning signs of certain psychopathologies, including anti-social personality disorder, also known as psychopathic personality disorder, is a history of torturing pets and small animals, a behavior known as zoosadism. According to the *New York Times*, "[t]he FBI has found that a history of cruelty to animals is one of the traits that regularly appears in its computer records of serial rapists and murderers, and the standard diagnostic and treatment manual for psychiatric and emotional disorders lists cruelty to animals a diagnostic criterion for conduct disorders. "A survey of psychiatric patients who had repeatedly tortured dogs and cats found all of them had high levels of aggression toward people as well, including one patient who had murdered a young boy." Robert K. Ressler, an agent with the Federal Bureau of Investigation's behavioral sciences unit, studied serial killers and noted,"Murderers like this (Jeffrey Dahmer) very often start out by killing and torturing animals as kids."

Cruelty to animals is one of the three components of the Macdonald triad, indicators of violent antisocial behavior in children and adolescents. According to the studies used to form this model, cruelty to animals is a common (but not with every case) behavior in children and adolescents who grow up to become serial killers and other violent criminals.

It has also been found that children who are cruel to animals have often witnessed or been victims of abuse themselves. In two separate studies cited by the Humane Society of the United States roughly one-third of families suffering from domestic abuse indicated that at least one child had hurt or killed a pet.

TV & film making

Animal cruelty has long been an issue with the art form of filmmaking, with even some big-budget Hollywood films receiving criticism for allegedly harmful—and sometimes lethal—treatment of animals during production. One of the most infamous examples of animal cruelty in film was Michael Cimino's legendary flop *Heaven's Gate*, in which numerous animals were brutalized and even killed during production. Cimino allegedly killed chickens and bled horses from the neck to gather samples of their blood to smear on actors for *Heaven's Gate*, and also allegedly had a horse blown up with dynamite while shooting a battle sequence, the shot of which made it into the film. After the release of the film *Reds*, the star and director of the picture, Warren Beatty apologized for his Spanish film crew's use of tripwires on horses while filming a battle scene, when Beatty wasn't present. Tripwires were used against horses when *Rambo III* and *The Thirteenth Warrior* were being filmed. An ox was sliced nearly in half during production of *Apocalypse Now*, while a donkey was bled to death for dramatic effect for the film *Manderlay*, in a scene later cut from the film.

Cruelty in film exists in movies outside the United States. There is a case of cruelty to animals in the South Korean film *The Isle*, according to its director Kim Ki-Duk. In the film, a real frog is skinned alive while fish are mutilated. Several animals were killed for the camera in the controversial Italian film *Cannibal Holocaust*. The images in the film include the slow and graphic beheading and ripping apart of a turtle, a monkey being beheaded and its brains being consumed by natives and a spider being chopped apart. In fact, *Cannibal Holocaust* was only one film in a collective of similarly themed movies (cannibal films) that featured unstaged animal cruelty. Their influences were rooted in the films of Mondo filmmakers, which sometimes contained similar content. In several countries, such as the UK, *Cannibal Holocaust* was only allowed for release with most of the animal cruelty edited out.

More recently, the video sharing site YouTube has been criticized for hosting thousands of videos of real life animal cruelty, especially the feeding of one animal to another for the purposes of entertainment and spectacle. Although some of these videos have been flagged as inappropriate by users, YouTube has generally declined to remove them, unlike videos which include copyright infringement.

The Screen Actors Guild (SAG) has contracted with the American Humane Association (AHA) for monitoring of animal use during filming or while on the set. Compliance with this arrangement is voluntary and only applies to films made in the United States. Films monitored by the American Humane Association may bear one of their end-credit messages. Many productions, including those made in the US, do not advise AHA or SAG of animal use in films, so there is no oversight.

Simulations of animal cruelty exist on television, too. On the September 23, 1999 edition of WWE Smackdown!, a plot line had professional wrestler Big Boss Man trick fellow wrestler Al Snow into appearing to eat his pet chihuahua Pepper.

Circuses

The use of animals in the circus has been controversial since animal welfare groups have documented instances of animal cruelty during the training of performing animals. The Humane Society of the United States has documented multiple cases of abuse and neglect, and cite several reasons for opposing the use of animals in circuses, including confining enclosures, lack of regular veterinary care, abusive training methods and lack of oversight by regulating bodies. Animal trainers have argued that some criticism is not based in fact, including beliefs that animals are 'hurt' by being shouted at, that caging is cruel and common, and the harm caused by the use of whips, chains or training implements.

In 2009, Bolivia passed legislation banning the use of any animals, wild or domestic, in circuses. The law states that circuses "constitute an act of cruelty." Circus operators had one year from the bill's passage on July 1, 2009 to comply.

In 2010, Lebanese animal rights groups became enraged when it was learned that wild performing animals belonging to the Monte Carlo Circus were transported from Egypt to Lebanon without being provided with food and water.

Restrictions

Following the campaign, new regulations were enacted that prohibit the use of animals in circuses in Israel. Finland and Singapore have restricted the use of animals in entertainment. The UK and Scottish Parliaments have committed to ban certain wild animals in travelling circuses and approximately 200 local authorities in the UK have banned all animal acts on council land.[citation needed] Animal acts are still very popular throughout much of Europe, the Americas and Asia. In the United States animal welfare standards are overseen by the United States Department of Agriculture under provisions of the Animal Welfare Act. Efforts to ban circus animals in cities like Denver, Colorado have been rejected by voters. Some circuses now present animal-free acts.

Crush films

Main article: Crush film

Animal snuff films, known as crush films can be found on the Internet. These films depict instances of animal cruelty, and/or pornographic acts with animals, usually involving the crushing death of an animal, including insects, mice, rats, guinea pigs, hamsters, monkeys, birds, cats, and dogs. In 1999, the U.S. government banned the depiction of animal cruelty, however the law was overturned by the 3rd U.S. Circuit Court of Appeals which ruled that the category "depiction of animal cruelty" contained in the law was not an exception to First Amendment protections. In an 8–1 decision handed down in April 2010, the U.S. Supreme Court agreed with the lower court's ruling, but on the grounds that the law was unconstitutionally broad. The case itself did not involve crush films, but rather, a video that in part depicted dogfighting.

Warfare

Military animals are creatures that have been employed by humankind for use in warfare. They are a specific application of working animals. Examples include horses, dogs and dolphins. Only recently has the involvement of animals in war been questioned, and practices such as using animals for fighting, as living bombs (as in the use of exploding donkeys) or for military testing purposes (such as during the Bikini atomic experiments) may now be criticised for being cruel. Princess Royal, the patron of the British Animals in War Memorial, stated that animals adapt to what humans want them to do, but that they will not do things that they don't

A horse with a gas mask during World War I

want to, despite training. Animal participation in human conflict was commemorated in the United Kingdom in 2004 with the erection of the Animals in War Memorial in Hyde Park, London.

In 2008 a video of a US Marine throwing a puppy over a cliff during the Iraq conflict was popularised as an internet phenomenon and attracted widespread criticism of the soldier's actions for being an act of cruelty.

Further reading

- Arluke, Arnold. *Brute Force: Animal Police and the Challenge of Cruelty*, Purdue University Press (August 15, 2004), hardcover, 175 pages, ISBN 1-55753-350-4. An ethnographic study of humane law enforcement officers.
- Lea, Suzanne Goodney (2007). *Delinquency and Animal Cruelty: Myths and Realities about Social Pathology*, hardcover, 168 pages, ISBN 978-1-59332-197-0. Lea challenges the argument made by animal rights activists that animal cruelty enacted during childhood is a precursor to human-directed violence.
- Munro H. (*The battered pet*) (1999) In F. Ascione & P. Arkow (Eds.) Child Abuse, Domestic Violence, and Animal Abuse. West Lafayette, IN: Purdue University Press, 199–208.

External links

- Goldfish used in art, to highlight morality, court finds no basis of cruelty (2003) [1] From BBC News
- Iditarod Organizers Hear Testimony of Alleged Dog Abuse [2] from FOX news
- *Four-legged Forensics: What Forensic Nurses Need to Know and Do About Animal Cruelty* [3] from Forensic Nursing magazine
- Cruelty toward Cats: Changing Perspectives [4] from The State of the Animals III: 2005 [5] ISBN 0-9748400-5-X
- Pet-Abuse.Com – Database of Criminal Animal Cruelty Cases [6]

The History and Basics of Animal Testing

Animal testing

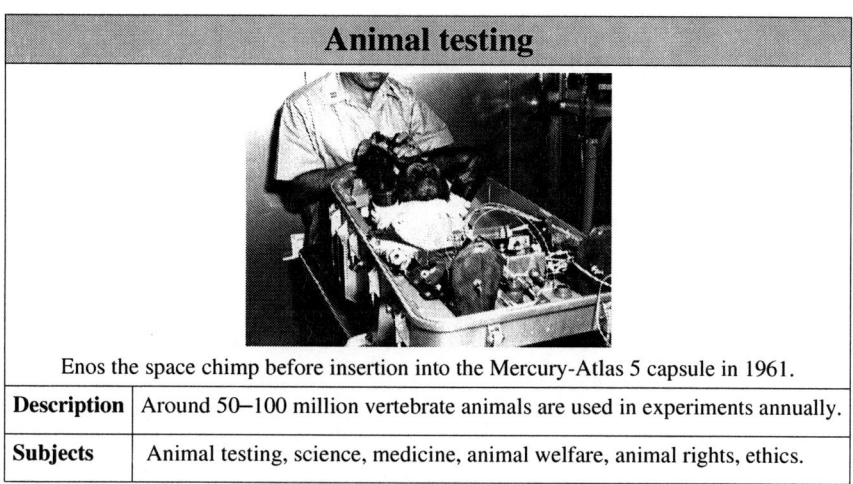

	Animal testing
	Enos the space chimp before insertion into the Mercury-Atlas 5 capsule in 1961.
Description	Around 50–100 million vertebrate animals are used in experiments annually.
Subjects	Animal testing, science, medicine, animal welfare, animal rights, ethics.

Animal testing, also known as **animal experimentation**, **animal research**, and **in vivo testing**, is the use of non-human animals in experiments. Worldwide it is estimated that 50 to 100 million vertebrate animals are used annually—from zebrafish to non-human primates. Invertebrates, mice, rats, birds, fish, frogs, and animals not yet weaned are not included in the figures; one estimate of mice and rats used in the United States alone in 2001 was 80 million. Most animals are euthanized after being used in an experiment. Sources of laboratory animals vary between countries and species; most animals are purpose-bred, while others are caught in the wild or supplied by dealers who obtain them from auctions and pounds.

The research is conducted inside universities, medical schools, pharmaceutical companies, farms, defense establishments, and commercial facilities that provide animal-testing services to industry. It includes pure research such as genetics, developmental biology, behavioural studies, as well as applied research such as biomedical research, xenotransplantation, drug testing and toxicology tests, including cosmetics testing. Animals are also used for education, breeding, and defense research. The practice is regulated to various degrees in different countries.

Supporters of the use of animals in experiments, such as the British Royal Society, argue that virtually every medical achievement in the 20th century relied on the use of animals in some way, with the

Institute for Laboratory Animal Research of the U.S. National Academy of Sciences arguing that even sophisticated computers are unable to model interactions between molecules, cells, tissues, organs, organisms, and the environment, making animal research necessary in many areas. A number of scientists, animal welfare, and animal rights organizations—such as PETA and BUAV—question the legitimacy of it, arguing that it is cruel, poor scientific practice, poorly regulated, that medical progress is being held back by misleading animal models, that some of the tests are outdated, that it cannot reliably predict effects in humans, that the costs outweigh the benefits, or that animals have an intrinsic right not to be used for experimentation.

Definitions

The terms animal testing, **animal experimentation**, animal research, *in vivo* **testing**, and **vivisection** have similar denotations but different connotations. Literally, "vivisection" means the "cutting up" of a living animal, and historically referred only to experiments that involved the dissection of live animals. The term is occasionally used to refer pejoratively to any experiment using living animals; for example, the *Encyclopædia Britannica* defines "vivisection" as: "Operation on a living animal for experimental rather than healing purposes; more broadly, all experimentation on live animals", although dictionaries point out that the broader definition is "used only by people who are opposed to such work". The word has a negative connotation, implying torture, suffering, and death. The word "vivisection" is preferred by those opposed to this research, whereas scientists typically use the term "animal experimentation".

History

Main article: History of animal testing

The earliest references to animal testing are found in the writings of the Greeks in the second and fourth centuries BCE. Aristotle (Ἀριστοτέλης) (384–322 BCE) and Erasistratus (304–258 BCE) were among the first to perform experiments on living animals. Galen, a physician in second-century Rome, dissected pigs and goats, and is known as the "father of vivisection." Avenzoar, an Arabic physician in twelfth-century Moorish Spain who also practiced dissection, introduced animal testing as an experimental method of testing surgical procedures before applying them to human patients.

An Experiment on a Bird in an Air Pump, from 1768, by Joseph Wright

Animals have been used repeatedly through the history of biomedical research. In the 1880s, Louis Pasteur convincingly demonstrated the germ theory of medicine by inducing anthrax in sheep. In the 1890s, Ivan Pavlov famously used dogs to describe classical conditioning. Insulin was first isolated from dogs in 1922, and revolutionized the treatment of diabetes. On November 3, 1957, a Russian dog, Laika, became the first of many animals to orbit the earth. In the 1970s, antibiotic treatments and vaccines for leprosy were developed using armadillos, then given to humans. The ability of humans to change the genetics of animals took a large step forwards in 1974 when Rudolf Jaenisch was able to produce the first transgenic mammal, by integrating DNA from the SV40 virus into the genome of mice. This genetic research progressed rapidly and, in 1996, Dolly the sheep was born, the first mammal to be cloned from an adult cell.

Toxicology testing became important in the 20th century. In the 19th century, laws regulating drugs were more relaxed. For example, in the U.S., the government could only ban a drug after a company had been prosecuted for selling products that harmed customers. However, in response to the Elixir Sulfanilamide disaster of 1937 in which the eponymous drug killed more than 100 users, the U.S. congress passed laws that required safety testing of drugs on animals before they could be marketed. Other countries enacted similar legislation. In the 1960s, in reaction to the Thalidomide tragedy, further laws were passed requiring safety testing on pregnant animals before a drug can be sold.

Historical debate

Claude Bernard, regarded as the "prince of vivisectors" argued that experiments on animals are "entirely conclusive for the toxicology and hygiene of man".

As the experimentation on animals increased, especially the practice of vivisection, so did criticism and controversy. In 1655, the advocate of Galenic physiology Edmund O'Meara said that "the miserable torture of vivisection places the body in an unnatural state." O'Meara and others argued that animal physiology could be affected by pain during vivisection, rendering results unreliable. There were also objections on an ethical basis, contending that the benefit to humans did not justify the harm to animals. Early objections to animal testing also came from another angle — many people believed that animals were inferior to humans and so different that results from animals could not be applied to humans.

On the other side of the debate, those in favor of animal testing held that experiments on animals were necessary to advance medical and biological knowledge. Claude Bernard, known as the "prince of vivisectors" and the father of physiology—whose wife, Marie Françoise Martin, founded the first anti-vivisection society in France in 1883—famously wrote in 1865 that "the science of life is a superb and dazzlingly lighted hall which may be reached only by passing through a long and ghastly kitchen". Arguing that "experiments on animals ... are entirely conclusive for the toxicology and hygiene of man...the effects of these substances are the same on man as on animals, save for differences in degree," Bernard established animal experimentation as part of the standard scientific method.

In 1896, the physiologist and physician Dr. Walter B. Cannon said "The antivivisectionists are the second of the two types Theodore Roosevelt described when he said, 'Common sense without conscience may lead to crime, but conscience without common sense may lead to folly, which is the handmaiden of crime.' " These divisions between pro- and anti- animal testing groups first came to public attention during the brown dog affair in the early 1900s, when hundreds of medical students clashed with anti-vivisectionists and police over a memorial to a vivisected dog.

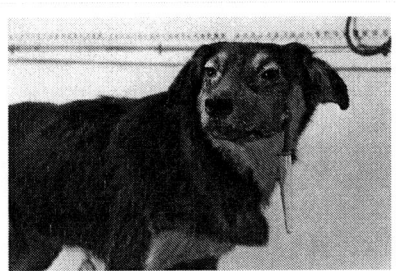

One of Pavlov's dogs with a saliva-catch container and tube surgically implanted in his muzzle, Pavlov Museum, 2005

In 1822, the first animal protection law was enacted in the British parliament, followed by the Cruelty to Animals Act (1876), the first law specifically aimed at regulating animal testing. The legislation was promoted by Charles Darwin, who wrote to Ray Lankester in March 1871: "You ask about my opinion on vivisection. I quite agree that it is justifiable for real investigations on physiology; but not for mere damnable and detestable curiosity. It is a subject which makes me sick with horror, so I will not say another word about it, else I shall not sleep to-night." Opposition to the use of animals in medical research first arose in the United States during the 1860s, when Henry Bergh founded the American Society for the Prevention of Cruelty to Animals (ASPCA), with America's first specifically anti-vivisection organization being the American AntiVivisection Society (AAVS), founded in 1883. Antivivisectionists of the era generally believed the spread of mercy was the great cause of civilization, and vivisection was cruel. However, in the USA the antivivisectionists' efforts were defeated in every legislature, overwhelmed by the superior organization and influence of the medical community. Overall, this movement had little legislative success until the passing of the Laboratory Animal Welfare Act, in 1966.

Care and use of animals

See also: Animal testing regulations, Institutional Animal Care and Use Committee, and Animals (Scientific Procedures) Act 1986

Regulations

The regulations that apply to animals in laboratories vary across species. In the U.S., under the provisions of the Animal Welfare Act and the *Guide for the Care and Use of Laboratory Animals* (the *Guide*), published by the National Academy of Sciences, any procedure can be performed on an animal if it can be successfully argued that it is scientifically justified. In general, researchers are required to consult with the institution's veterinarian and its Institutional Animal Care and Use Committee (IACUC), which every research facility is obliged to maintain. The IACUC must ensure that alternatives, including non-animal alternatives, have been considered, that the experiments are not unnecessarily duplicative, and that pain relief is given unless it would interfere with the study. Larry Carbone, a laboratory animal veterinarian, writes that, in his experience, IACUCs take their work very seriously regardless of the species involved, though the use of non-human primates always raises what he calls a "red flag of special concern." A study published in *Science* magazine in July 2001 confirmed the low reliability of IACUC reviews of animal experiments. Funded by the National Science Foundation, the three-year study found that animal-use committees that do not know the specifics of the university and personnel do not make the same approval decisions as those made by animal-use committees that do know the university and personnel. Specifically, blinded committees more often ask for more information rather than approving studies.

The IACUCs regulate all vertebrates in testing at institutions receiving federal funds in the USA. Although the provisions of the Animal Welfare Act do not include purpose-bred rodents and birds, these species are equally regulated under Public Health Service policies that govern the IACUCs. Animal Welfare Act regulations are enforced by the USDA, whereas Public Health Service regulations are enforced by OLAW and in many cases by AAALAC.

Numbers

Accurate global figures for animal testing are difficult to obtain. The British Union for the Abolition of Vivisection (BUAV) estimates that 100 million vertebrates are experimented on around the world every year, 10–11 million of them in the European Union. The Nuffield Council on Bioethics reports that global annual estimates range from 50 to 100 million animals. None of the figures include invertebrates such as shrimp and fruit flies. Animals bred for research then killed as surplus, animals used for breeding purposes, and animals not yet weaned are also not included in the figures.

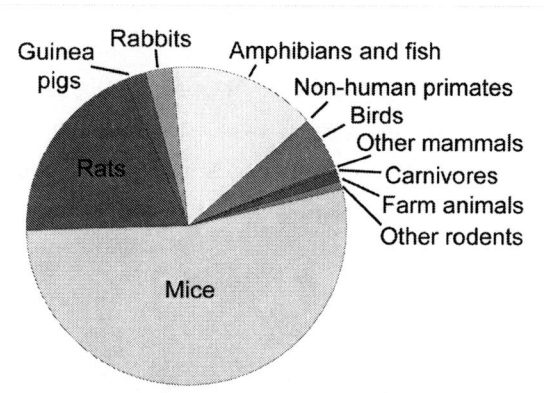

Types of vertebrates used in animal testing in Europe in 2005: a total of 12.1 million animals were used.

According to the U.S. Department of Agriculture (USDA), the total number of animals used in that country in 2005 was almost 1.2 million, but this does not include rats and mice, which make up about 90% of research animals. In 1995, researchers at Tufts University Center for Animals and Public Policy estimated that 14–21 million animals were used in American laboratories in 1992, a reduction from a high of 50 million used in 1970. In 1986, the U.S. Congress Office of Technology Assessment reported that estimates of the animals used in the U.S. range from 10 million to upwards of 100 million each year, and that their own best estimate was at least 17 million to 22 million.

In the UK, Home Office figures show that 3.2 million procedures were carried out in 2007, a rise of 189,500 since the previous year. Four thousand procedures used non-human primates, down 240 from 2006. A "procedure" refers to an experiment that might last minutes, several months, or years. Most animals are used in only one procedure: animals either die because of the experiment or are euthanized afterwards.

Species

Invertebrates

Main article: Animal testing on invertebrates

Although many more invertebrates than vertebrates are used, these experiments are largely unregulated by law. The most used invertebrate species are *Drosophila melanogaster*, a fruit fly, and *Caenorhabditis elegans*, a nematode worm. In the case of *C. elegans*, the worm's body is completely transparent and the precise lineage of all the organism's cells is known, while studies in the fly *D. melanogaster* can use an amazing array of genetic tools. These animals offer great advantages over vertebrates, including their short life cycle and the ease with which large numbers may be

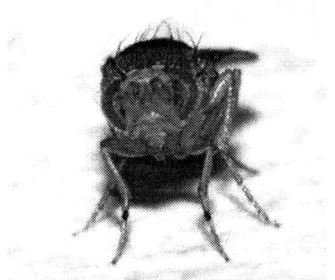

Fruit flies are commonly used.

studied, with thousands of flies or nematodes fitting into a single room. However, the lack of an adaptive immune system and their simple organs prevent worms from being used in medical research such as vaccine development. Similarly, flies are not widely used in applied medical research, as their immune system differs greatly from that of humans, and diseases in insects can be very different from diseases in vertebrates.

Vertebrates

A white Wistar lab rat

Further information: Animal testing on frogs, Animal testing on rabbits, Animal testing on rodents, Draize test, and Median lethal dose

In the U.S., the numbers of rats and mice used is estimated at 20 million a year. Other rodents commonly used are guinea pigs, hamsters, and gerbils. Mice are the most commonly used vertebrate species because of their size, low cost, ease of handling, and fast reproduction rate. Mice are widely considered to be the best model of inherited human disease and share 99% of their genes with humans. With the advent of genetic engineering technology, genetically modified mice can be generated to order and can provide models for a range of human diseases. Rats are also widely used for physiology, toxicology and cancer research, but genetic manipulation is much harder in rats than in mice, which limits the use of these rodents in basic science. Nearly 200,000 fish and 20,000 amphibians were used in the UK in 2004. The main species used is the zebrafish, *Danio rerio*, which are translucent during their embryonic stage, and the African clawed frog, *Xenopus laevis*. Over 20,000 rabbits were used for animal testing in the UK in 2004. Albino rabbits are used in eye irritancy tests because rabbits have less tear flow than other animals, and the lack of eye pigment in albinos make the effects easier to visualize. Rabbits are also frequently used for the production of polyclonal antibodies.

Cats and dogs

See also: Laika and Russian space dogs

Cats are most commonly used in neurological research. Over 25,500 cats were used in the U.S. in 2000, around half of whom were used in experiments which, according to the American Anti-Vivisection Society, had the potential to cause "pain and/or distress".

Dogs are widely used in biomedical research, testing, and education — particularly beagles, because they are gentle and easy to handle. They are commonly used as models for human diseases in cardiology, endocrinology, and bone and joint studies, research that tends to be highly invasive, according to the Humane Society of the United States. The U.S. Department of Agriculture's Animal Welfare Report for 2005 shows that 66,000 dogs were used in USDA-registered facilities in that year. In the U.S., some of the dogs are purpose-bred, while most are supplied by so-called Class B dealers licensed by the USDA to buy animals from auctions, shelters, newspaper ads, and who are sometimes accused of stealing pets.

Non-human primates

Main article: Animal testing on non-human primates

Non-human primates (NHPs) are used in toxicology tests, studies of AIDS and hepatitis, studies of neurology, behavior and cognition, reproduction, genetics, and xenotransplantation. They are caught in the wild or purpose-bred. In the U.S. and China, most primates are domestically purpose-bred, whereas in Europe the majority are imported purpose-bred. Rhesus monkeys, cynomolgus monkeys, squirrel monkeys, and owl monkeys are imported; around 12,000 to 15,000 monkeys are imported into the U.S. annually. In total, around 70,000 NHPs are used each year in the United States and European Union. Most of the NHPs used are macaques; but marmosets, spider monkeys, and squirrel monkeys are also used, and baboons and chimpanzees are used in the U.S; in 2006 there were 1133 chimpanzees in U.S. primate centers. The first transgenic primate was produced in 2001, with the development of a method that could introduce new genes into a rhesus macaque. This transgenic technology is now being applied in the search for a treatment for the genetic disorder Huntington's disease. Notable studies on non-human primates have been part of the polio vaccine development, and development of Deep Brain Stimulation, and their current heaviest non-toxicological use occurs in the monkey AIDS model, SIV. In 2008 a proposal to ban all primates experiments in the EU has sparked a vigorous debate.

Sources

Main articles: Laboratory animal sources and International trade in primates

Animals used by laboratories are largely supplied by specialist dealers. Sources differ for vertebrate and invertebrate animals. Most laboratories breed and raise flies and worms themselves, using strains and mutants supplied from a few main stock centers. For vertebrates, sources include breeders who supply purpose-bred animals; businesses that trade in wild animals; and dealers who supply animals sourced from pounds, auctions, and newspaper ads. Animal shelters also supply the laboratories directly. Large centers also exist to distribute strains of genetically-modified animals; the National Institutes of Health *Knockout Mouse Project*, for example, aims to provide knockout mice for every gene in the mouse genome.

In the U.S., Class A breeders are licensed by the U.S. Department of Agriculture (USDA) to sell animals for research purposes, while Class B dealers are licensed to buy animals from "random sources" such as auctions, pound seizure, and newspaper ads. Some Class B dealers have been accused of kidnapping pets and illegally trapping strays, a practice known as *bunching*. It was in part out of public concern over the sale of pets to research facilities that the 1966 Laboratory Animal Welfare Act was ushered in — the Senate Committee on Commerce reported in 1966 that stolen pets had been retrieved from Veterans Administration facilities, the Mayo Institute, the University of Pennsylvania, Stanford University, and Harvard and Yale Medical Schools. The USDA recovered at least a dozen stolen pets during a raid on a Class B dealer in Arkansas in 2003.

Four states in the U.S. — Minnesota, Utah, Oklahoma, and Iowa — require their shelters to provide animals to research facilities. Fourteen states explicitly prohibit the practice, while the remainder either allow it or have no relevant legislation.

In the European Union, animal sources are governed by *Council Directive 86/609/EEC*, which requires lab animals to be specially bred, unless the animal has been lawfully imported and is not a wild animal or a stray. The latter requirement may also be exempted by special arrangement. In the UK, most animals used in experiments are bred for the purpose under the 1988 Animal Protection Act, but wild-caught primates may be used if exceptional and specific justification can be established. The United States also allows the use of wild-caught primates; between 1995 and 1999, 1,580 wild baboons were imported into the U.S. Over half the primates imported between 1995 and 2000 were handled by Charles River Laboratories, Inc., or by Covance, which is the single largest importer of primates into the U.S.

Pain and suffering

Further information: Animal cognition and Pain in animals

The extent to which animal testing causes pain and suffering, and the capacity of animals to experience and comprehend them, is the subject of much debate.

According to the U.S. Department of Agriculture, in 2006 about 670,000 animals (57%) (not including rats, mice, birds, or invertebrates) were used in procedures that did not include more than momentary pain or distress. About 420,000 (36%) were used in procedures in which pain or distress was relieved by anesthesia, while 84,000 (7%) were used in studies that would cause pain or distress that would not be relieved.

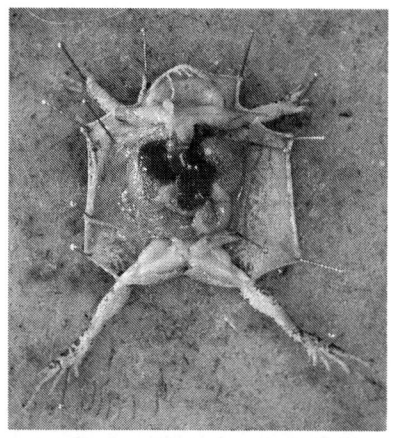

Prior to vivisection for educational purposes, chloroform was administered to this common sand frog to induce terminal anesthesia.

In the UK, research projects are classified as mild, moderate, and substantial in terms of the suffering the researchers conducting the study say they may cause; a fourth category of "unclassified" means the animal was anesthetized and killed without recovering consciousness, according to the researchers. In December 2001, 1,296 (39%) of project licenses in force were classified as mild, 1,811 (55%) as moderate, 63 (2%) as substantial, and 139 (4%) as unclassified. There have, however, been suggestions of systemic underestimation of procedure severity.

The idea that animals might not feel pain as human beings feel it traces back to the 17th-century French philosopher, René Descartes, who argued that animals do not experience pain and suffering because they lack consciousness. Bernard Rollin of Colorado State University, the principal author of two U.S. federal laws regulating pain relief for animals, writes that researchers remained unsure into the 1980s as to whether animals experience pain, and that veterinarians trained in the U.S. before 1989 were simply taught to ignore animal pain. In his interactions with scientists and other veterinarians, he was regularly asked to "prove" that animals are conscious, and to provide "scientifically acceptable" grounds for claiming that they feel pain. Carbone writes that the view that animals feel pain differently is now a minority view. Academic reviews of the topic are more equivocal, noting that although the argument that animals have at least simple conscious thoughts and feelings has strong support, some critics continue to question how reliably animal mental states can be determined. The ability of invertebrate species of animals, such as insects, to feel pain and suffering is also unclear.

The defining text on animal welfare regulation, "Guide for the Care and Use of Laboratory Animals" defines the parameters that govern animal testing in the USA. It states "The ability to experience and respond to pain is widespread in the animal kingdom...Pain is a stressor and, if not relieved, can lead to unacceptable levels of stress and distress in animals." The Guide states that the ability to recognize the symptoms of pain in different species is vital in efficiently applying pain relief and that it is essential for the people caring for and using animals to be entirely familiar with these symptoms. On the subject of analgesics used to relieve pain, the Guide states "The selection of the most appropriate analgesic or anesthetic should reflect professional judgment as to which best meets clinical and humane requirements without compromising the scientific aspects of the research protocol". Accordingly, all issues of animal pain and distress, and their potential treatment with analgesia and anesthesia, are required regulatory issues in receiving animal protocol approval.

Euthanasia

Further information: Euthanasia and Animal euthanasia

There is general agreement that animal life should not be taken wantonly, and regulations require that scientists use as few animals as possible. However, while policy makers consider suffering to be the central issue and see animal euthanasia as a way to reduce suffering, others, such as the RSPCA, argue that the lives of laboratory animals have intrinsic value. Regulations focus on whether particular methods cause pain and suffering, not whether their death is undesirable in itself. The animals are euthanized at the end of studies for sample collection or post-mortem examination; during studies if their pain or suffering falls into certain categories regarded as unacceptable, such as depression, infection that is unresponsive to treatment, or the failure of large animals to eat for five days; or when they are unsuitable for breeding or unwanted for some other reason.

Methods of euthanizing laboratory animals are chosen to induce rapid unconsciousness and death without pain or distress. The methods that are preferred are those published by councils of veterinarians. The animal can be made to inhale a gas, such as carbon monoxide and carbon dioxide, by being placed in a chamber, or by use of a face mask, with or without prior sedation or anesthesia. Sedatives or anesthetics such as barbiturates can be given intravenously, or inhalant anesthetics may be used. Amphibians and fish may be immersed in water containing an anesthetic such as tricaine. Physical methods are also used, with or without sedation or anesthesia depending on the method. Recommended methods include decapitation (beheading) for small rodents or rabbits. Cervical dislocation (breaking the neck or spine) may be used for birds, mice, and immature rats and rabbits. Maceration (grinding into small pieces) is used on 1 day old chicks. High-intensity microwave irradiation of the brain can preserve brain tissue and induce death in less than 1 second, but this is currently only used on rodents. Captive bolts may be used, typically on dogs, ruminants, horses, pigs and rabbits. It causes death by a concussion to the brain. Gunshot may be used, but only in cases where a penetrating captive bolt may not be used. Some physical methods are only acceptable after the animal is unconscious. Electrocution may be used for cattle, sheep, swine, foxes, and mink after the animals are unconscious, often by a prior electrical stun. Pithing (inserting a tool into the base of the brain) is usable on animals already unconscious. Slow or rapid freezing, or inducing air embolism are acceptable only with prior anesthesia to induce unconsciousness.

Research classification

Pure research

Basic or pure research investigates how organisms behave, develop, and function. Those opposed to animal testing object that pure research may have little or no practical purpose, but researchers argue that it may produce unforeseen benefits, rendering the distinction between pure and applied research—research that has a specific practical aim—unclear. Pure research uses larger numbers and a greater variety of animals than applied research. Fruit flies, nematode worms, mice and rats together account for the vast majority, though small numbers of other species are used, ranging from sea slugs through to armadillos. Examples of the types of animals and experiments used in basic research include:

- Studies on *embryogenesis* and *developmental biology*. Mutants are created by adding transposons into their genomes, or specific genes are deleted by gene targeting. By studying the changes in development these changes produce, scientists aim to understand both how organisms normally develop, and what can go wrong in this process. These studies are particularly powerful since the basic controls of development, such as the homeobox genes, have similar functions in organisms as diverse as fruit flies and man.

- Experiments into *behavior*, to understand how organisms detect and interact with each other and their environment, in which fruit flies, worms, mice, and rats are all widely used. Studies of brain function, such as memory and social behavior, often use rats and birds. For some species, behavioral research is combined with enrichment strategies for animals in captivity because it allows them to engage in a wider range of activities.

- Breeding experiments to study *evolution* and *genetics*. Laboratory mice, flies, fish, and worms are inbred through many generations to create strains with defined characteristics. These provide animals of a known genetic background, an important tool for genetic analyses. Larger mammals are rarely bred specifically for such studies due to their slow rate of reproduction, though some scientists take advantage of inbred domesticated animals, such as dog or cattle breeds, for comparative purposes. Scientists studying how animals evolve use many animal species to see how variations in where and how an organism lives (their niche) produce adaptations in their physiology and morphology. As an example, sticklebacks are now being used to study how many and which types of mutations are selected to produce adaptations in animals' morphology during the evolution of new species.

Applied research

Applied research aims to solve specific and practical problems. Compared to pure research, which is largely academic in origin, applied research is usually carried out in the pharmaceutical industry, or by universities in commercial partnerships. These may involve the use of animal models of diseases or conditions, which are often discovered or generated by pure research programmes. In turn, such applied studies may be an early stage in the drug discovery process. Examples include:

- Genetic modification of animals to study disease. Transgenic animals have specific genes inserted, modified or removed, to mimic specific conditions such as single gene disorders, such as Huntington's disease. Other models mimic complex, multifactorial diseases with genetic components, such as diabetes, or even transgenic mice that carry the same mutations that occur during the development of cancer. These models allow investigations on how and why the disease develops, as well as providing ways to develop and test new treatments. The vast majority of these transgenic models of human disease are lines of mice, the mammalian species in which genetic modification is most efficient. Smaller numbers of other animals are also used, including rats, pigs, sheep, fish, birds, and amphibians.

- Studies on models of naturally occurring disease and condition. Certain domestic and wild animals have a natural propensity or predisposition for certain conditions that are also found in humans. Cats are used as a model to develop immunodeficiency virus vaccines and to study leukemia because their natural predisposition to FIV and Feline leukemia virus. Certain breeds of dog suffer from narcolepsy making them the major model used to study the human condition. Armadillos and humans are among only a few animal species that naturally suffer from leprosy; as the bacteria responsible for this disease cannot yet be grown in culture, armadillos are the primary source of bacilli used in leprosy vaccines.

- Studies on induced animal models of human diseases. Here, an animal is treated so that it develops pathology and symptoms that resemble a human disease. Examples include restricting blood flow to the brain to induce stroke, or giving neurotoxins that cause damage similar to that seen in Parkinson's disease. Such studies can be difficult to interpret, and it is argued that they are not always comparable to human diseases. For example, although such models are now widely used to study Parkinson's disease, the British anti-vivisection interest group BUAV argues that these models only superficially resemble the disease symptoms, without the same time course or cellular pathology. In contrast, scientists assessing the usefulness of animal models of Parkinson's disease, as well as the medical research charity *The Parkinson's Appeal*, state that these models were invaluable and that they led to improved surgical treatments such as pallidotomy, new drug treatments such as levodopa, and later deep brain stimulation.

Xenotransplantation

Main article: Xenotransplantation

Xenotransplantation research involves transplanting tissues, or organs from one species to another, as a way to overcome the shortage of human organs for use in organ transplants. Current research involves using primates as the recipients of organs from pigs that have been genetically-modified to reduce the primates' immune response against the pig tissue. Although transplant rejection remains a problem, recent clinical trials that involved implanting pig insulin-secreting cells into diabetics did reduce these people's need for insulin.

The British Home Office released figures in 1999 showing that 270 monkeys had been used in xenotransplantation research in Britain during the previous four years. Documents leaked from Huntingdon Life Sciences to *The Observer* in 2003 showed, between 1994 and 2000, wild baboons were imported to the UK from Africa to be used in experiments that involved grafting pigs' hearts and kidneys onto the primates' necks, abdomens, and chests. *The Observer* reports that some baboons died after suffering strokes, vomiting, diarrhea, and paralysis, while others died *en route* to the UK. The experiments were conducted by Imutran Ltd, a subsidiary of Novartis Pharma AG in conjunction with Cambridge University and Huntingdon Life Sciences. Novartis told the newspaper that developing new cures for humans invariably means experimenting on live animals. The newspaper also wrote that researchers were deliberately underestimating the suffering in order to obtain licences. A report from Imutran said: "The Home Office will attempt to get the kidney transplants classified as 'moderate,' ensuring that it is easier for Imutran to receive a licence and ignoring the 'severe' nature of these programmes."

Toxicology testing

Main article: Toxicology testing

Further information: Draize test, LD50, Acute toxicity, and Chronic toxicity

Toxicology testing, also known as safety testing, is conducted by pharmaceutical companies testing drugs, or by contract animal testing facilities, such as Huntingdon Life Sciences, on behalf of a wide variety of customers. According to 2005 EU figures, around one million animals are used every year in Europe in toxicology tests; which are about 10% of all procedures. According to *Nature*, 5,000 animals are used for each chemical being tested, with 12,000 needed to test pesticides. The tests are conducted without anesthesia, because interactions between drugs can affect how animals detoxify chemicals, and may interfere with the results.

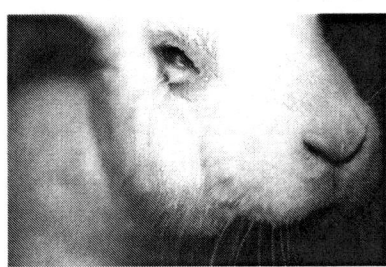
A rabbit during a Draize test

Toxicology tests are used to examine finished products such as pesticides, medications, food additives, packing materials, and air freshener, or their chemical ingredients. Most tests involve testing ingredients rather than finished products, but according to BUAV, manufacturers believe these tests overestimate the toxic effects of substances; they therefore repeat the tests using their finished products to obtain a less toxic label.

The substances are applied to the skin or dripped into the eyes; injected intravenously, intramuscularly, or subcutaneously; inhaled either by placing a mask over the animals and restraining them, or by placing them in an inhalation chamber; or administered orally, through a tube into the stomach, or simply in the animal's food. Doses may be given once, repeated regularly for many months, or for the lifespan of the animal.[*citation needed*]

There are several different types of acute toxicity tests. The LD50 ("Lethal Dose 50%") test is used to evaluate the toxicity of a substance by determining the dose required to kill 50% of the test animal population. This test was removed from OECD international guidelines in 2002, replaced by methods such as the fixed dose procedure, which use fewer animals and cause less suffering. *Nature* writes that, as of 2005, "the LD50 acute toxicity test ... still accounts for one-third of all animal [toxicity] tests worldwide." Irritancy can be measured using the Draize test, where a test substance is applied to an animal's eyes or skin, usually an albino rabbit. For Draize eye testing, the test involves observing the effects of the substance at intervals and grading any damage or irritation, but the test should be halted and the animal killed if it shows "continuing signs of severe pain or distress". The Humane Society of the United States writes that the procedure can cause redness, ulceration, hemorrhaging, cloudiness, or even blindness. This test has also been criticized by scientists for being cruel and inaccurate, subjective, over-sensitive, and failing to reflect human exposures in the real world. Although no accepted *in vitro* alternatives exist, a modified form of the Draize test called the *low volume eye test* may reduce suffering and provide more realistic results and this was adopted as the new standard in September 2009. However, the Draize test will still be used for substances that are not severe irritants.

The most stringent tests are reserved for drugs and foodstuffs. For these, a number of tests are performed, lasting less than a month (acute), one to three months (subchronic), and more than three months (chronic) to test general toxicity (damage to organs), eye and skin irritancy, mutagenicity, carcinogenicity, teratogenicity, and reproductive problems. The cost of the full complement of tests is several million dollars per substance and it may take three or four years to complete.

These toxicity tests provide, in the words of a 2006 United States National Academy of Sciences report, "critical information for assessing hazard and risk potential". *Nature* reported that most animal tests either over- or underestimate risk, or do not reflect toxicity in humans particularly well, with false positive results being a particular problem. This variability stems from using the effects of high doses of chemicals in small numbers of laboratory animals to try to predict the effects of low doses in large numbers of humans. Although relationships do exist, opinion is divided on how to use data on one species to predict the exact level of risk in another.

Cosmetics testing

Main article: Testing cosmetics on animals

Cosmetics testing on animals is particularly controversial. Such tests, which are still conducted in the U.S., involve general toxicity, eye and skin irritancy, phototoxicity (toxicity triggered by ultraviolet light) and mutagenicity.

Cosmetics testing is banned in the Netherlands, Belgium, and the UK, and in 2002, after 13 years of discussion, the European Union (EU) agreed to phase in a near-total ban on the sale of animal-tested cosmetics throughout the EU from 2009, and to ban all cosmetics-related animal testing. France, which is home to the world's largest cosmetics company, L'Oreal, has protested the proposed ban by lodging a case at the European Court of Justice in Luxembourg, asking that the ban be quashed. The ban is also opposed by the European Federation for Cosmetics Ingredients, which represents 70 companies in Switzerland, Belgium, France, Germany and Italy.

Drug testing

Before the early 20th century, laws regulating drugs were lax. Currently, all new pharmaceuticals undergo rigorous animal testing before being licensed for human use. Tests on pharmaceutical products involve:

- *metabolic tests*, investigating pharmacokinetics – how drugs are absorbed, metabolized and excreted by the body when introduced orally, intravenously, intraperitoneally, intramuscularly, or transdermally.
- *toxicology tests*, which gauge acute, sub-acute, and chronic toxicity. Acute toxicity is studied by using a rising dose until signs of toxicity become apparent. Current European legislation demands that "acute toxicity tests must be carried out in two or more mammalian species" covering "at least two different routes of administration". Sub-acute toxicity is where the drug is given to the animals for four to six weeks in doses below the level at which it causes rapid poisoning, in order to discover if any toxic drug metabolites build up over time. Testing for chronic toxicity can last up to two years and, in the European Union, is required to involve two species of mammals, one of which must be non-rodent.
- *efficacy studies*, which test whether experimental drugs work by inducing the appropriate illness in animals. The drug is then administered in a double-blind controlled trial, which allows researchers to determine the effect of the drug and the dose-response curve.
- Specific tests on *reproductive function*, *embryonic toxicity*, or *carcinogenic potential* can all be required by law, depending on the result of other studies and the type of drug being tested.

Education, breeding, and defense

Animals are also used for education and training; are bred for use in laboratories; and are used by the military to develop weapons, vaccines, battlefield surgical techniques, and defensive clothing. For example, in 2008 the United States Defense Advanced Research Projects Agency used live pigs to study the effects of improvised explosive device explosions on internal organs, especially the brain.

There are efforts in many countries to find alternatives to using animals in education. Horst Spielmann, German director of the Central Office for Collecting and Assessing Alternatives to Animal Experimentation, while describing Germany's progress in this area, told German broadcaster ARD in 2005: "Using animals in teaching curricula is already superfluous. In many countries, one can become a doctor, vet or biologist without ever having performed an experiment on an animal."

Ethics

Background

Further information: Animal welfare and Animal rights

The ethical questions raised by performing experiments on animals are subject to much debate, and viewpoints have shifted significantly over the 20th century. There remain disagreements about which procedures are useful for which purposes, as well as disagreements over which ethical principles apply to which species. The dominant ethical position worldwide is that achievement of scientific and medical goals using animal testing is desirable, so long as animal suffering and use is minimized. The British government has additionally required that the cost to animals in an experiment be weighed against the gain in knowledge. Some medical schools and agencies in China, Japan, and South Korea have built cenotaphs for killed animals. In Japan there are also annual memorial services (*Ireisai* 慰□祭) for animals sacrificed at medical school.

A wide range of minority viewpoints exist. The view that animals have moral rights (animal rights) is a philosophical position proposed by Tom Regan, among others, who argues that animals are beings with beliefs and desires, and as such are the "subjects of a life" with moral value and therefore moral rights. Regan still sees ethical differences between killing human and non-human animals, and argues that to save the former it is permissible to kill the latter. Others, such as Bernard Rollin, argue that benefits to human beings cannot outweigh animal suffering, and that human beings have no moral right to use an animal in ways that do not benefit that individual. Another prominent position is that of philosopher Peter Singer, who argues that there are no grounds to include a being's species in considerations of whether their suffering is important in utilitarian moral considerations.

Although these arguments have not been widely accepted, governments such as the Netherlands and New Zealand have responded to the concerns by outlawing invasive experiments on certain classes of non-human primates, particularly the great apes.

Prominent cases

Various specific cases of animal testing have drawn attention, including both instances of beneficial scientific research, and instances of alleged ethical violations by those performing the tests.

Muscle physiology

The fundamental properties of muscle physiology were determined with on work done using frog muscles (including the force generating mechanism of all muscle, the length-tension relationship, and the force-velocity curve), and frogs are still the preferred model organism due to the long survival of muscles in vitro and the possibility of isolating intact single-fiber preparations (not possible in other organisms). Modern physical therapy and the understanding and treatment of muscular disorders is based on this work and subsequent work in mice (often engineered to express disease states such as muscular dystrophy).

University of California, Riverside

Main article: Britches (monkey)

1985 was a pivotal year in the debate about animal research in the United States, with the enactment of amendments to the Animal Welfare Act. Britches, a macaque monkey, was born that year inside the University of California, Riverside, removed from his mother at birth, and left alone with his eyelids sewn shut, and a sonar sensor on his head, as part of an experiment to test sensory substitution devices for blind people. The Animal Liberation Front raided the laboratory on April 20, 1985, removing Britches and 466 other animals, and reportedly inflicting $700,000-worth of damage to equipment. A spokesman for the university said the allegations of mistreatment were false, and that the raid caused long-term damage to its research projects. The National Institutes of Health conducted an eight-month investigation and concluded that no corrective action was necessary.

Huntingdon Life Sciences

Main article: Stop Huntingdon Animal Cruelty

In 1997, People for the Ethical Treatment of Animals filmed staff inside Huntingdon Life Sciences (HLS) in the UK, Europe's largest animal-testing facility, hitting puppies, shouting at them, and simulating sex acts while taking blood samples. The company said the employees were dismissed. Two pleaded guilty to "cruelly terrifying dogs," and were given community service orders and ordered to pay £250 costs, the first lab technicians to have been prosecuted for animal cruelty in the UK. The broadcast of the video on Britain's Channel 4 Television in March 1997 triggered the formation of Stop Huntingdon Animal Cruelty (SHAC), an international leaderless resistance campaign to close HLS, which has been criticized for its sometimes violent tactics. In January 2009, several British SHAC activists were jailed for blackmailing companies linked to HLS.

Roslin Institute

Main article: Dolly (sheep)

Dolly the sheep: the first clone produced from an adult animal

In February 1997 a team at the Roslin Institute in Scotland announced the birth of Dolly the sheep, a ewe that had been cloned from tissue taken from another adult sheep. Dolly was produced through nuclear transfer to an unfertilised oocyte, and was the only lamb that survived from 277 attempts at this technique. Dolly appeared to be a normal sheep, living for six years and giving birth to several lambs, but was euthanized in 2003 after contracting a progressive lung disease. Although the production of Dolly was a scientific breakthrough, it was controversial, since it showed that not only could cloned animals be produced for use in farming, but also that it would now be, in principle, possible to clone a human being.

University of Cambridge

Main article: Primate experiments at Cambridge University

The British Union for the Abolition of Vivisection (BUAV) raised concerns about primate experiments at the University of Cambridge in 2002. In a series of court cases, the BUAV alleged that monkeys had undergone surgery to induce a stroke, and were left alone after the procedure for 15 hours overnight. Researchers had trained the monkeys to perform certain tasks before inflicting brain damage and re-testing them. The monkeys were only given food and water for two hours a day, to encourage them to perform the tasks. The judge hearing BUAV's application for a judicial review rejected the allegation that the Home Secretary had been negligent in granting the university a license. The British government's chief inspector of animals conducted a review of the facilities and experiments. It concluded the veterinary input at Cambridge was "exemplary"; the facility "seems adequately staffed"; and the animals afforded "appropriate standards of accommodation and care."

Columbia University

Main article: Primate experiments at Columbia University

CNN reported in October 2003 that Catherine Dell'Orto, a veterinarian at Columbia University, had approached the university's Institute of Comparative Medicine about the treatment of baboons who were undergoing surgery as part of an experiment into stroke treatment. She said the baboons, who were in some cases having an eyeball removed, were left to suffer in their cages after the surgery. She alleged there was systemic maltreatment, poor record-keeping, and other violations of regulations, according to CNN. She presented her evidence in October 2002 and, dissatisfied with the response, contacted People for the Ethical Treatment of Animals two months later.

In March 2003, a lab technician shot video inside the lab, which according to *The New York Daily News* showed primates in cages without pain medication; the video included one baboon with a metal cylinder screwed into its head, according to the newspaper. Dell'Orto told the newspaper that primates were often not euthanized or given painkillers after surgery; she said other primates had torn their fingers off out of fear. The U.S. Department of Agriculture upheld Dell'Orto's complaint that there was shoddy record-keeping, and that 11 animals had been provided with "inadequate or questionable care." They found no evidence that the experiments violated federal guidelines or that there had been retaliation against Dell'Orto. CNN reported that Columbia responded by ordering better record-keeping, a review of the veterinary care program, and tighter criteria for euthanasia of laboratory animals.

Covance

Main article: Covance

In 2004, German journalist Friedrich Mülln shot undercover footage of staff in Covance, Münster, Europe's largest primate-testing center, making monkeys dance in time to blaring pop music, handling them roughly, and screaming at them. The monkeys were kept isolated in small wire cages with little or no natural light, no environmental enrichment, and high noise levels from staff shouting and playing the radio (video). Primatologist Jane Goodall described the living conditions of the monkeys as horrendous. Another primatologist, Stephen Brend, told BUAV that using monkeys in such a stressed state is bad science, and trying to extrapolate useful data in such circumstances is what he called an untenable proposition. In 2004 and 2005, PETA shot footage inside the company in the United States. According to *The Washington Post*, PETA said an employee of the group filmed primates being choked, hit, and denied medical attention when badly injured. The U.S. Department of Agriculture fined Covance $8,720 for 16 citations, three of which involved lab monkeys; the other citations involved administrative issues and equipment.

Threats to researchers

In 2006, a primate researcher at the University of California, Los Angeles (UCLA) shut down the experiments in his lab after threats from animal rights activists. The researcher had received a grant to use 30 macaque monkeys for vision experiments; each monkey was anesthetized for a single physiological experiment lasting up to 120 hours, and then euthanized. The researcher's name, phone number, and address were posted on the website of the Primate Freedom Project. Demonstrations were held in front of his home. A Molotov cocktail was placed on the porch of what was believed to be the home of another UCLA primate researcher; instead, it was accidentally left on the porch of an elderly woman unrelated to the university. The Animal Liberation Front claimed responsibility for the attack. As a result of the campaign, the researcher sent an email to the Primate Freedom Project stating "you win," and "please don't bother my family anymore." In another incident at UCLA in June 2007, the Animal Liberation Brigade placed a bomb under the car of a UCLA children's ophthalmologist who experiments on cats and rhesus monkeys; the bomb had a faulty fuse and did not detonate. UCLA is now refusing Freedom of Information Act requests for animal medical records.

These attacks, as well as similar incidents that caused the Southern Poverty Law Center to declare in 2002 that the animal rights movement had "clearly taken a turn toward the more extreme," this prompted the US government to pass the Animal Enterprise Terrorism Act and the UK government to add the offense of "Intimidation of persons connected with animal research organisation" to the Serious Organised Crime and Police Act 2005. Such legislation, and the arrest and imprisonment of extremists may have decreased the incidence of attacks.

Alternatives to animal testing

Main article: Alternatives to animal testing

Scientists and governments state that animal testing should cause as little suffering to animals as possible, and that animal tests should only be performed where necessary. The "three Rs" are guiding principles for the use of animals in research in most countries:

1. **Replacement** refers to the preferred use of non-animal methods over animal methods whenever it is possible to achieve the same scientific aim.
2. **Reduction** refers to methods that enable researchers to obtain comparable levels of information from fewer animals, or to obtain more information from the same number of animals.
3. **Refinement** refers to methods that alleviate or minimize potential pain, suffering or distress, and enhance animal welfare for the animals still used.

Although such principles have been welcomed as a step forwards by some animal welfare groups, they have also been criticized as both outdated by current research, and of little practical effect in improving animal welfare.

See also

- Bateson's cube
- Human subject research
- Krogh's principle
- Preclinical imaging
- The People's Petition

Further reading and external links

- Conn, P. Michael and Parker, James V (2008). The Animal Research War, Palgrave Macmillan, ISBN 978-0-230-60014-0
- Guerrini, Anita (2003). *Experimenting with humans and animals: from Galen to animal rights*. Baltimore: The Johns Hopkins University Press. ISBN 0-8018-7197-2.
- Stephens, Martin & Rowan, Andrew. "An overview of animal testing" [1]PDF (129 KB), Humane Society of the United States, accessed October 29, 2005
- 1940 American/Soviet film of dog resurrection experiments [2]

- "Select Committee on Animals In Scientific Procedures Report" [3], Select Committee on Animals in Scientific Procedures, British House of Lords, July 16, 2002, accessed October 27, 2005.
- "Statistics of Scientific Procedures on Living Animals" [4], Great Britain, 2004.
- "Why use animals?" [5] and other FAQ, North Carolina Association for Biomedical Research, accessed October 23, 2005
- "Basic statement" [6], Aërzte gegen Tierversuche (Doctors against Animal Experiments), accessed October 23, 2005.
- "Biomed for the layperson" [7], Laboratory Primate Advocacy Group, accessed February 24, 2006.
- In Focus "Animal Experiments in Research" (German Reference Centre for Ethics in the Life Sciences) [8]
- Encyclopedia of Earth: Animal testing alternatives [9]
- Go3R: semantic search to avoid animal experiments [10]

History of animal testing

For the history of ethics in animal rights, see Animal rights.

The **history of animal testing** goes back to the writings of the Greeks in the third and 4th centuries BCE, with Aristotle (384-322 BCE) and Erasistratus (304-258 BCE) among the first to perform experiments on living animals. Galen, a physician in 2nd-century Rome, dissected pigs and goats, and is known as the "father of vivisection." Avenzoar, an Arabic physician in 12th-century Moorish Spain who also practiced dissection, introduced animal testing as an experimental method of testing surgical procedures before applying them to human patients.

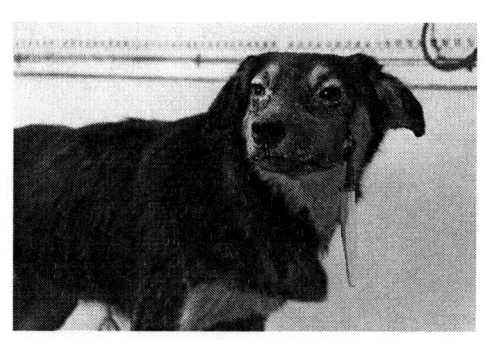

One of Pavlov's dogs with a saliva-catch container and tube surgically implanted in his muzzle. Pavlov Museum, 2005

Early Debate

Animal testing

Main articles
Animal testing
Alternatives to animal testing
Testing on: invertebrates
frogs · primates
rabbits · rodents
Animal testing regulations
History of animal testing
History of model organisms
IACUC
Laboratory animal sources
Pain and suffering in lab animals
Testing cosmetics on animals
Toxicology testing
Vivisection

Issues
Biomedical Research
Animal rights/Animal welfare
Animals (Scientific Procedures)
Great ape research ban
International trade in primates

Controversial experiments
Britches · Brown Dog affair
Cambridge University primates
Pit of despair
Silver Spring monkeys
Unnecessary Fuss

Companies
Charles River Laboratories, Inc.
Covance · Harlan
Huntingdon Life Sciences
UK lab animal suppliers
Nafovanny · Shamrock

Groups/campaigns
AALAS · AAAS · ALF
Americans for Medical Progress
Boyd Group · BUAV
Dr Hadwen Trust
Foundation for Biomedical
Research · FRAME
National Anti-Vivisection
Society
PETA · Physicians Committee
for Responsible Medicine
Primate Freedom Project
Pro-Test
SPEAK · SHAC
Speaking of Research
Understanding Animal Research

Writers/activists
Tipu Aziz · Michael Balls
Neal Barnard · Colin Blakemore
Simon Festing · Gill Langley
Ingrid Newkirk · Bernard Rollin
Jerry Vlasak

Categories
Animal testing · Animal rights
Animal welfare

Related templates
Template:Animal rights

In 1655, physiologist Edmund O'Meara is recorded as saying that "the miserable torture of vivisection places the body in an unnatural state." O'Meara thus expressed one of the chief scientific objections to vivisection: that the pain that the subject endured would interfere with the accuracy of the results.

In 1822, the first animal protection law was enacted in the British parliament, followed by the Cruelty to Animals Act (1876), the first law specifically aimed at regulating animal testing. The legislation was promoted by Charles Darwin, who wrote to Ray Lankester in March 1871:

> You ask about my opinion on vivisection. I quite agree that it is justifiable for real investigations on physiology; but not for mere damnable and detestable curiosity. It is a subject which makes me sick with horror, so I will not say another word about it, else I shall not sleep to-night."

Opposition to the use of animals in medical research arose in the United States during the 1860s, when Henry Bergh founded the American Society for the Prevention of Cruelty to Animals (ASPCA), with America's first specifically anti-vivisection organization being the American AntiVivisection Society (AAVS), founded in 1883.

In the UK, an article in the *Medical Times and Gazette* on April 28, 1877, indicates that anti-vivisectionist campaigners, mainly clergymen, had prepared a number of posters entitled, "This is vivisection," "This is a living dog," and "This is a living rabbit," depicting animals in a poses that they said copied the work of Elias von Cyon in St. Petersburg, though the article says the images differ from the originals. It states that no more than 10 or a dozen men were actively involved in animal testing on living animals in the UK at that time.

Antivivisectionists of the era generally believed the spread of mercy was the great cause of civilization, and vivisection was cruel. However, in the U.S., the antivivisectionists' efforts were defeated in every legislature, overwhelmed by the superior organization and influence of the medical community. The early antivivisectionist movement in the U.S. dwindled greatly in the 1920s, potentially caused by a variety of factors including opposition of the medical community, improvement in medicine through the use of animals, and the tendency of the antivivisectionists to misrepresentation and exaggeration, and their use of inaccurate, vague and outdated references. Overall, this movement had no US legislative success until the passing of the Laboratory Animal Welfare Act, in 1966.

On the other side of the debate, those in favor of animal testing held that experiments on animals were necessary to advance medical and biological knowledge. Claude Bernard, known as the "prince of vivisectors" and the father of physiology — whose wife, Marie Françoise Martin, founded the first anti-vivisection society in France in 1883 — famously wrote in 1865 that "the science of life is a superb and dazzlingly lighted hall which may be reached only by passing through a long and ghastly kitchen". Arguing that "experiments on animals ... are entirely conclusive for the toxicology and hygiene of man...the effects of these substances are the same on man as on animals, save for differences in degree," Bernard established animal experimentation as part of the standard scientific method. In 1896, the physiologist and physician Dr. Walter B. Cannon said "The antivivisectionists are the second of the two types Theodore Roosevelt described when he said, 'Common sense without conscience may lead to crime, but conscience without common sense may lead to folly, which is the handmaiden of crime.' " These divisions between pro- and anti- animal testing groups first came to public attention during the brown dog affair in the early 20th century, when hundreds of medical students clashed with anti-vivisectionists and police over a memorial to a vivisected dog.

Basic science advances

In 1242, Ibn al-Nafis provided accurate descriptions of the circulation of blood in mammals. A more complete description of this circulation was later provided in the 17th century by William Harvey. In the 18th century, Antoine Lavoisier, used a guinea pig in a calorimeter to prove that respiration was a form of combustion, and Stephen Hales measured blood pressure in the horse. In the 1780s, Luigi Galvani demonstrated that electricity applied to a dead, dissected, frog's leg muscle caused it to twitch, which led to an appreciation for the relationship between electricity and animation. In the 1880s, Louis Pasteur convincingly demonstrated the germ theory of medicine by giving anthrax to sheep. In the

1890s, Ivan Pavlov famously used dogs to describe classical conditioning.

In 1921 Otto Loewi provided the first strong evidence that neuronal communication with target cells occurred via chemical synapses. He extracted two hearts from frogs and left them beating in an ionic bath. He stimulated the attached Vagus nerve of the first heart, and observed its beating slowed. When the second heart was placed in the ionic bath of the first, it also slowed.

In the 1920s, Edgar Adrian formulated the theory of neural communication that the frequency of action potentials, and not the size of the action potentials, was the basis for communicating the magnitude of the signal. His work was performed in an isolated frog nerve-muscle preparation. Adrian was awarded a Nobel Prize for his work.

In the 1960s David Hubel and Torsten Wiesel demonstrated the macrocolumnar organization of visual areas in cats and monkeys, and provided physiological evidence for the critical period for the development of disparity sensitivity in vision (i.e.: the main cue for depth perception), and were awarded a Nobel Prize for their work.

In 1996 Dolly the sheep was born, the first mammal to be cloned from an adult cell.

Medical advances

In the 1880s and 1890s, Emil von Behring isolated the diphtheria toxin and demonstrated its effects in guinea pigs. He went on to demonstrate immunity against diphtheria in animals in 1898 by injecting a mix of toxin and antitoxin. This work constituted in part the rationale for awarding von Behring the 1901 Nobel Prize in Physiology and Medicine. Roughly 15 years later, Behring announced such a mix suitable for human immunity which largely banished the diphtheria from the scourges of mankind. The antitoxin is famously commemorated each year in the Iditarod race, which is modeled after the delivery of diphtheria antitoxin to Nome in the 1925 serum run to Nome. The success of the animal studies in producing the diphtheria antitoxin are attributed by some as a cause in the decline of the early 20th century antivivisectionist movement in the USA.

In 1921, Frederick Banting tied up the pancreatic ducts of dogs, and discovered that the isolates of pancreatic secretion could be used to keep dogs with diabetes alive. He followed up these experiments with chemical isolation of insulin in 1922 with John Macleod. These experiments used bovine sources instead of dogs to improve the supply. The first person treated was Leonard Thompson, a 14 year old diabetic who only weighed 65 pounds and was about to slip into a coma and die. After the first dose, the formulation had to be re-worked, a process that took 12 days. The second dose was effective. These two won the Nobel Prize in Physiology or Medicine in 1923 for their discovery of insulin and its treatment of diabetes mellitus. Thompson lived 13 more years taking insulin. Before insulin's clinical use, a diagnosis of diabetes mellitus meant death; Thompson had been diagnosed in 1919.

In the 1943, Selman Waksman's laboratory discovered streptomycin using a series of screens to find antibacterial substances from the soil. Waksman coined the term antibiotic with regards to these substances. Waksman would win the Nobel Prize in Medicine in 1952 for his discoveries in antibiotics. Corwin Hinshaw and William Feldman took the streptomycin samples and cured tuberculosis in four guinea pigs with it. Hinshaw followed these studies with human trials that provided a dramatic advance in the ability to stop and reverse the progression of tuberculosis. Mortality from tuberculosis in the UK has diminished from the early 20th century due to better hygiene and improved living standards, but from the moment antibiotics were introduced, the fall became much steeper, so that by the 1980s mortality in developed countries was effectively zero.

In the 1940s, Jonas Salk used Rhesus monkey cross-contamination studies to isolate the three forms of the polio virus that affected hundreds of thousands yearly. Salk's team created a vaccine against the strains of polio in cell cultures of Rhesus monkey kidney cells. The vaccine was made publicly available in 1955, and reduced the incidence of polio 15-fold in the USA over the following five years. Albert Sabin made a superior "live" vaccine by passing the polio virus through animal hosts, including monkeys. The vaccine was produced for mass consumption in 1963 and is still in use today. It had virtually eradicated polio in the USA by 1965. It has been estimated that 100,000 Rhesus monkeys were killed in the course of developing the polio vaccines, and 65 doses of vaccine were produced for each monkey.

Also in the 1940s, John Cade tested lithium salts in guinea pigs in a search for pharmaceuticals with anticonvulsant properties. The animals seemed calmer in their mood. He then tested lithium on himself, before using it to treat recurrent mania. The introduction of lithium revolutionized the treatment of manic-depressives by the 1970s. Prior to Cade's animal testing, manic-depressives were treated with lobotomy or electro-convulsive therapy.

In the 1950s the first safer, non-volatile anaesthetic halothane was developed through studies on rodents, rabbits, dogs, cats and monkeys. This paved the way for a whole new generation of modern general anaesthetics - also developed by animal studies - without which modern, complex surgical operations would be virtually impossible.

In 1960, Albert Starr pioneered heart valve replacement surgery in humans after a series of surgical advances in dogs. He received the Lasker Medical Award in 2007 for his efforts, along with Alain Carpentier. In 1968 Carpentier made heart valve replacements from the heart valves of pigs, which are pre-treated with gluteraldehyde to blunt immune response. Over 300,000 people receive heart valve replacements derived from Starr and Carpentier's designs annually. Carpentier said of Starr's initial advances "Before his prosthetic, patients with valvular disease would die".

In the 1970s, leprosy multi-drug antibiotic treatments were refined using leprosy bacteria grown in armadillos, and were then tested in human clinical trials. Today, the nine-banded armadillo is still used to culture the bacteria that causes leprosy, for studies of the proteomics and genomics (the genome was completed in 1998) of the bacteria, for the purposes of improving therapy and developing vaccines. Leprosy is still prevalent in Brazil, Madagascar, Mozambique, Tanzania, India and Nepal, with over 400,000 cases at the beginning of 2004. The bacteria has not yet been cultured *in vitro* with success necessary to develop drug treatments or vaccines, and mice and armadillos have been the sources of the bacteria for research.

The non-human primate models of AIDS, using HIV-2, SHIV, and SIV in macaques, have been used as a complement to ongoing research efforts against the virus. The drug tenofovir has had its efficacy and toxicology evaluated in macaques, and found longterm-highdose treatments had adverse effects not found using shortterm-highdose treatment followed by longterm-lowdose treatment. This finding in macaques was translated into human dosing regimens. Prophylactic treatment with anti-virals has been evaluated in macaques, because introduction of the virus can only be controlled in an animal model. The finding that prophylaxis can be effective at blocking infection has altered the treatment for occupational exposures, such as needle exposures. Such exposures are now followed rapidly with anti-HIV drugs, and this practice has resulted in measurable transient virus infection similar to the NHP model. Similarly, the mother-to-fetus transmission, and its fetal prophylaxis with antivirals such as tenofovir and AZT, has been evaluated in controlled testing in macaques not possible in humans, and this knowledge has guided antiviral treatment in pregnant mothers with HIV. "The comparison and correlation of results obtained in monkey and human studies is leading to a growing validation and recognition of the relevance of the animal model. Although each animal model has its limitations, carefully designed drug studies in nonhuman primates can continue to advance our scientific knowledge and guide future clinical trials."

Throughout the 20th century, research that used live animals has led to many other medical advances and treatments for human diseases, such as: organ transplant techniques and anti-transplant rejection medications, the heart-lung machine, antibiotics like penicillin, and whooping cough vaccine.

Presently, animal experimentation continues to be used in research that aims to solve medical problems from Alzheimer's disease, multiple sclerosis spinal cord injury, and many more conditions in which there is no useful *in vitro* model system available.

Veterinary advances

A veterinary surgeon at work with a cat.

Animal testing for veterinary studies accounts for around five per cent of research using animals. Treatments to each of the following animal diseases have been derived from animal studies: rabies, anthrax, glanders, Feline immunodeficiency virus (FIV), tuberculosis, Texas cattle fever, Classical swine fever (hog cholera), Heartworm and other parasitic infections.

Basic and applied research in veterinary medicine continues in varied topics, such as searching for improved treatments and vaccines for feline leukemia virus and improving veterinary oncology.

See also

- History of model organisms
- Animal testing
- Alarik Frithiof Holmgren

Animal Rights and Laws

Animal law

Animal liberation

Main articles
Animal rights
Animal liberation movement
Animal law

Issues

Animal Enterprise Terrorism Act
Animal testing
Bile bear • Blood sport
Covance • Draize test
Factory farming • Fur trade
Great Ape research ban • HLS
Lab animal sources • LD50
Meat • Nafovanny • Open rescue
Operation Backfire • Primate trade
Seal hunting • Speciesism • Veganism

Cases

Britches • Brown Dog affair
Cambridge • Pit of despair
Silver Spring monkeys
Unnecessary Fuss

Notable writers
Carol Adams • Jeremy Bentham
Steven Best • Stephen Clark
Gary Francione • Gill Langley
Mary Midgley • Tom Regan
Bernard Rollin • Richard Ryder
Henry Salt • Peter Singer
Steven Wise • Roger Yates

Notable activists
Greg Avery • David Barbarash
Mel Broughton • Rod Coronado
Barry Horne • Ronnie Lee
Keith Mann • Ingrid Newkirk
Heather Nicholson • Jill Phipps
Craig Rosebraugh • Henry Spira
Andrew Tyler • Jerry Vlasak
Paul Watson • Robin Webb

Notable groups/campaigns
List of animal rights groups
Animal Aid • ALDF • ALF • BUAV
GAP • Hunt Saboteurs • PETA • PCRM
Sea Shepherd • SPEAK • SHAC

Political parties
List of animal advocacy parties
Animal Alliance • Animals Count
Animal Protection Party
PACMA
Party for the Animals
Tierschutzpartei

Books and magazines
AR books • AR magazines
Animal Liberation
Arkangel • *Bite Back*
No Compromise

Films
Animal rights films
Behind the Mask • *Earthlings*
The Animals Film
Peaceable Kingdom • *Unnecessary Fuss*

Related categories
ALF • Animal testing
Animal law • Animal rights
AR movement • Blood sports
Livestock • Meat
Poultry

Related templates
Rights • Animal testing
Agriculture • Fishing

Animal law is a combination of statutory and case law in which the nature – legal, social or biological – of nonhuman animals is an important factor. Animal law encompasses companion animals, wildlife, animals used in entertainment and animals raised for food and research. The emerging field of animal law is often analogized to the environmental law movement 30 years ago.

Approaches to animal law

Animal law issues encompass a broad spectrum of approaches—from philosophical explorations of the rights of animals to pragmatic discussions about the rights of those who use animals, who has standing to sue when an animal is harmed in a way that violates the law, and what constitutes legal cruelty. Animal law permeates and affects most traditional areas of the law – including tort, contract, criminal and constitutional law. Examples of this intersection include:

- Animal custody disputes in divorce or separations.
- Veterinary malpractice cases.
- Housing disputes involving "no pets" policies and discrimination laws.
- Damages cases involving the wrongful death or injury to a companion animal.
- Enforceable trusts for companion being adopted by states across the country.
- Criminal law encompassing domestic violence and anti-cruelty laws.

Animal law organizations

A growing number of state and local bar associations now have animal law committees. The Animal Legal Defense Fund was founded by attorney Joyce Tischler in 1979 as the first organization dedicated to promoting the field of animal law and using the law to protect the lives and defend the interests of animals.

In the Swiss canton of Zurich an animal lawyer, Antoine Goetschel, is employed by the canton government to represent the interests of animals in animal cruelty cases. In this capacity, he attempts to insure that the Swiss animal protection laws, which are among the strictest in the world, are correctly enforced.

Animal law in academia

Animal law has been taught in at least 119 law schools in the U.S., including Harvard, Stanford, UCLA, Northwestern, University of Michigan and Duke and is currently taught in at least 117 schools. Animal law is also currently taught in 7 law schools in Canada. In the U.S. there are Student Animal Legal Defense Fund (SALDF) chapters in 132 law schools, with an additional seven chapters in Canada. SALDF chapters are student groups that are affiliated with the Animal Legal Defense Fund and share its mission to protect the lives and advance the interests of animals through the legal system.

The comprehensive animal law casebook is, co-authored by Sonia S. Waisman, Bruce A. Wagman, and Pamela D. Frasch. Because animal law is not a traditional legal field, most of the book's chapters are framed in terms of familiar subsets of law such as tort, contract, criminal and constitutional law. Each chapter sets out cases and commentary where animal law affects those broader areas.

The Animal Protection Laws of the United States of America & Canada compendium, by Stephan K. Otto, Director of Legislative Affairs for the Animal Legal Defense Fund, is a comprehensive animal protection laws collection. It contains a detailed survey of the general animal protection and related statutes for all of the states, principal districts and territories of the United States of America, and for all of Canada; along with full-text versions of each jurisdiction's laws.

See also

- Intrinsic value (animal ethics)
- Animal ethics
- *Animal Law Review*
- Animal Legal Defense Fund
- Animal welfare
- Animal Welfare Act
- Category:Animal rights and welfare legislation
- Brazilian Abolitionist Movement for Animal liberation
- Hunting Act 2004
- Society for Animal Protective Legislation

Bibliography

- "Animal Law: Yesterday and Today"[1] Bernstein, Robin, *New Jersey Lawyer*, p. 23, 27, August 2005.
- Animal law for "least protected" and "most innocent"[2], May 20, 2008, *The UW Daily*, Seattle
- "Fido, Fluffy Become More High Profile Part of Law,"[3] March 29, 2008, *USA Today*

External links

- Center for Animal Law Studies[4], Lewis & Clark Law School
- Animal Legal and Historical Center[5], Michigan State University College of Law
- Animal protection laws[6], Animal Legal Defense Fund
- International Institute for Animal Law[7], National Anti-Vivisection Society
- From The State of the Animals III: 2005[5], Humane Society of the United States

    International Animal Law, with a Concentration on Latin America, Asia, and Africa[8]

    Progress in Animal Legislation: Measurement and Assessment[9]

Animal rights

Animal rights	
Animal rights advocates argue that animals ought to be viewed as persons, not property.	
Description	Animals are members of the moral community.
Early proponents	Jeremy Bentham (1748–1832) Henry Salt (1851–1939)
Modern proponents	Peter Singer, Tom Regan, Gary Francione
Key texts	Salt's *Animals' Rights* [1] (1894) Singer's *Animal Liberation* (1972)
Subject	Philosophy, ethics

Animal rights, also referred to as **animal liberation**, is the idea that the most basic interests of non-human animals should be afforded the same consideration as the similar interests of human beings. Advocates approach the issue from different philosophical positions, but agree that animals should be viewed as non-human persons and members of the moral community, and should not be used as food, clothing, research subjects, or entertainment. They argue that human beings should stop seeing other sentient beings as property—not even as property to be treated kindly.

The idea of awarding rights to animals has the support of legal scholars such as Alan Dershowitz and Laurence Tribe of Harvard Law School, while Toronto lawyer Clayton Ruby argued in 2008 that the movement had reached the stage the gay rights movement was at 25 years earlier. Animal law is taught in 119 out of 180 law schools in the United States, in eight law schools in Canada, and is routinely covered in universities in philosophy or applied ethics courses.

Critics argue that animals are unable to enter into a social contract or make moral choices, and for that reason cannot be regarded as possessors of rights, a position summed up by the philosopher Roger Scruton, who writes that only humans have duties and therefore only humans have rights. A parallel argument is that there is nothing inherently wrong with using animals as resources so long there is no unnecessary suffering, a view known as the animal welfare position. There has also been criticism, including from within the animal rights movement itself, of certain forms of animal rights activism, in particular the destruction of fur farms and animal laboratories by the Animal Liberation Front.

Development of the idea

Moral status of animals in the ancient world

Main articles: Moral status of animals in the ancient world and Human exceptionalism

The 21st-century debates about how humans should treat animals can be traced to the ancient world. The idea that the use of animals by humans—for food, clothing, entertainment, and as research subjects—is morally acceptable, springs mainly from two sources. First, there is the idea of a divine hierarchy based on the theological concept of "dominion", from Genesis (1:20–28), where Adam is given "dominion over the fish of the sea, and over the fowl of the air, and over the cattle, and over all the earth, and over every creeping thing that creepeth upon the earth." Although the concept of dominion need not entail property rights, it has been interpreted over the centuries to imply ownership.

Michelangelo's The Creation of Adam. The Book of Genesis said God gave humankind "dominion" over non-humans.

There is also the idea that animals are inferior because they lack rationality and language, and as such are worthy of less consideration than humans, or even none. Springing from this is the idea that individual animals have no separate moral identity: a pig is simply an example of the class of pigs, and it is to the class, not to the individual, that human responsibility or stewardship applies. This leads to the argument that the use of individual animals is acceptable so long as the species is not threatened with extinction.

17th century: Animals as automata

1641: Descartes

Further information: Dualism (philosophy of mind) and Scientific Revolution

❝ [Animals] eat without pleasure, cry without pain, grow without knowing it; they desire nothing, fear nothing, know nothing.❞
— Nicolas Malebranche (1638–1715)

The year 1641 was significant for the idea of animal rights. The great influence of the century was the French philosopher, René Descartes (1596–1650), whose *Meditations* was published that year, and whose ideas about animals informed attitudes well into the 21st century.

Writing during the scientific revolution—a revolution of which he was one of the chief architects—Descartes proposed a mechanistic theory of the universe, the aim of which was to show that the world could be mapped out without allusion to subjective experience. The senses deceive, he wrote in the *First Meditation* in 1641, and "it is prudent never to trust wholly those who have deceived us even once."

> Hold then the same view of the dog which has lost his master, which has sought him in all the thoroughfares with cries of sorrow, which comes into the house troubled and restless, goes downstairs, goes upstairs; goes from room to room, finds at last in his study the master he loves, and betokens his gladness by soft whimpers, frisks, and caresses. There are barbarians who seize this dog, who so greatly surpasses man in fidelity and friendship, and nail him down to a table and dissect him alive, to show you the mesaraic veins! You discover in him all the same organs of feeling as in yourself. Answer me, mechanist, has Nature arranged all the springs of feeling in this animal to the end that he might not feel? — Voltaire (1694–1778)

His mechanistic approach was extended to the issue of animal consciousness. Mind, for Descartes, was a thing apart from the physical universe, a separate substance, linking human beings to the mind of God. The non-human, on the other hand, are nothing but complex automata, with no souls, minds, or reason. They can see, hear, and touch, but they are not, in any sense, conscious, and are unable to suffer or even to feel pain.

In the *Discourse*, published in 1637, Descartes wrote that the ability to reason and use language involves being able to respond in complex ways to "all the contingencies of life," something that animals clearly cannot do. He argued from this that any sounds animals make do not constitute language, but are simply automatic responses to external stimuli.

1635, 1641, 1654: First known laws protecting animals

Richard Ryder writes that the first known legislation against animal cruelty in the English-speaking world was passed in Ireland in 1635. It prohibited pulling wool off sheep, and the attaching of ploughs to horses' tails, referring to "the cruelty used to beasts," which Ryde writes is probably the earliest reference to this concept in the English language.

In 1641, the year Descartes' *Meditations* was published, the first legal code to protect domestic animals in North America was passed by the Massachusetts Bay Colony. The colony's constitution was based on *The Body of Liberties* by the Reverend Nathaniel Ward (1578–1652), a lawyer, Puritan clergyman, and University of Cambridge graduate, originally from Suffolk, England. Ward listed the "rites" the Colony's general court later endorsed, including rite number 92: "No man shall exercise any Tirrany or Crueltie toward any bruite Creature which are usuallie kept for man's use." Historian Roderick Nash writes that, at the height of Descartes' influence in Europe, it is significant that the early New Englanders created a law that implied animals were not unfeeling automata.

The Puritans passed animal protection legislation in England too. Katheen Kete of Trinity College, Hartford, Connecticut writes that animal welfare laws were passed in 1654 as part of the ordinances of the Protectorate—the government under Oliver Cromwell, which lasted 1653–1659—during the English Civil War. Cromwell disliked blood sports, particularly cockfighting, cock throwing, dog fighting, as well as bull baiting and bull running, both said to tenderize the meat. These could frequently be seen in towns, villages, in fairgrounds, and became associated for the Puritans with idleness, drunkenness, and gambling. Kete writes that the Puritans interpreted the dominion of man over animals in the Book of Genesis to mean responsible stewardship, rather than ownership. The opposition to blood sports became part of what was seen as Puritan interference in people's lives, which became a leitmotif of resistance to them, Kete writes, and the animal protection laws were overturned during the Restoration, when Charles II was returned to the throne in 1660. Bull baiting remained lawful in England for another 162 years, until it was outlawed in 1822.

1693: Locke

Against Descartes, the British philosopher John Locke (1632–1704) argued, in *Some Thoughts Concerning Education* in 1693, that animals do have feelings, and that unnecessary cruelty toward them is morally wrong, but—echoing Thomas Aquinas—the right not to be so harmed adhered either to the animal's owner, or to the person who was being harmed by being cruel, not to the animal itself. Discussing the importance of preventing children from tormenting animals, he wrote: "For the custom of tormenting and killing of beasts will, by degrees, harden their minds even towards men."

18th century: The centrality of sentience, not reason

1754: Rousseau

Jean-Jacques Rousseau (1712–1778) argued in Discourse on Inequality in 1754 that animals should be part of natural law, not because they are rational, but because they are sentient:

Jean-Jacques Rousseau argued in 1754 that animals are part of natural law, and have natural rights, because they are sentient.

> [Here] we put an end to the time-honoured disputes concerning the participation of animals in natural law: for it is clear that, being destitute of intelligence and liberty, they cannot recognize that law; as they partake, however, in some measure of our nature, in consequence of the sensibility with which they are endowed, they ought to partake of natural right; so that mankind is subjected to a kind of obligation even toward the brutes. It appears, in fact, that if I am bound to do no injury to my fellow-creatures, this is less because they are rational than because they are sentient beings: and this quality, being common both to men and beasts, ought to entitle the latter at least to the privilege of not being wantonly ill-treated by the former.

1785: Kant

> Animals ... are there merely as a means to an end. That end is man. — Immanuel Kant

The German philosopher Immanuel Kant (1724–1804), following Locke, opposed the idea that humans have duties toward non-humans. For Kant, cruelty to animals was wrong solely on the grounds that it was bad for humankind. He argued in 1785 that humans have duties only toward other humans, and that "cruelty to animals is contrary to man's duty to *himself*, because it deadens in him the feeling of sympathy for their sufferings, and thus a natural tendency that is very useful to morality in relation to other humans is weakened."

1789: Bentham

Four years later, one of the founders of modern utilitarianism, the English philosopher Jeremy Bentham (1748–1832), although deeply opposed to the concept of natural rights, argued with Rousseau that it was the ability to suffer, not the ability to reason, that should be the benchmark of how we treat other beings. If rationality were the criterion, many humans, including babies and disabled people, would also have to be treated as though they were things. He wrote in 1789, just as slaves were being freed by the French, but were still held captive in the British dominions:

Jeremy Bentham: "The time will come, when humanity will extend its mantle over every thing which breathes" (1781).

> The day has been, I grieve to say in many places it is not yet past, in which the greater part of the species, under the denomination of slaves, have been treated by the law exactly upon the same footing, as, in England for example, the inferior races of animals are still. The day *may* come when the rest of the animal creation may acquire those rights which never could have been witholden from them but by the hand of tyranny. The French have already discovered that the blackness of the skin is no reason a human being should be abandoned without redress to the caprice of a tormentor. It may one day come to be recognized that the number of the legs, the villosity of the skin, or the termination of the *os sacrum* are reasons equally insufficient for abandoning a sensitive being to the same fate. What else is it that should trace the insuperable line? Is it the faculty of reason or perhaps the faculty of discourse? But a full-grown horse or dog, is beyond comparison a more rational, as well as a more conversable animal, than an infant of a day or a week or even a month, old. But suppose the case were otherwise, what would it avail? the question is not, Can they *reason*?, nor Can they *talk*? but, Can they *suffer?*

1792: Thomas Taylor

Despite Rousseau and Bentham, the idea that animals did or ought to have rights remained ridiculous. When Mary Wollstonecraft (1759–1797), the British feminist writer, published *A Vindication of the Rights of Woman* in 1792, Thomas Taylor (1758—1835), a Cambridge philosopher, responded with an anonymous tract called *Vindication of the Rights of Brutes*, intended as a *reductio ad absurdum*. Taylor took Wollstonecraft's arguments, and those of Thomas Paine's *Rights of Man* (1790), and showed that they applied equally to animals, leading to the conclusion that animals have "intrinsic and real dignity and worth," a conclusion absurd enough, in his view, to discredit Wollstonecraft's and Paine's positions entirely.

19th century: Emergence of *jus animalium*

Legislation

The first known prosecution for cruelty to animals was brought in 1822 against two men found beating horses in London's Smithfield Market, where livestock had been sold since the 10th century. They were fined 20 shillings each.

Further information: Cruel Treatment of Cattle Act 1822, Cruelty to Animals Act 1835, Cruelty to Animals Act 1849, and Cruelty to Animals Act 1876

> What could be more innocent than bull baiting, boxing, or dancing? — George Canning, British Foreign Secretary in April 1800 in response to a bill to ban bull baiting.

Badger baiting was outlawed in England by the Cruelty to Animals Act 1835. Painting by Henry Thomas Alken, 1824

The 19th century saw an explosion of interest in animal protection, particularly in England. Debbie Legge and Simon Brooman of Liverpool John Moores University wrote that the educated classes became concerned about attitudes toward the old, the needy, children, and the insane, and that this concern was extended to non-humans. Before the 19th century, there had been prosecutions for poor treatment of animals, but only because of the damage to the animal as property. In 1793, for example, John Cornish was found not guilty of maiming a horse after pulling its tongue out, the judge ruling that he could be found guilty only if there was evidence of malice toward the owner.

From 1800 onwards, there were several attempts in England to introduce animal welfare or rights legislation. The first was a bill in 1800 against bull baiting, introduced by Sir William Pulteney, and opposed by the Secretary at War, William Windham, on the grounds that it was anti-working class. Another attempt was made in 1802 by William Wilberforce, again opposed by Windham, who said that the Bill was supported by Methodists and Jacobins who wished, for different reasons, to "destroy the Old English character, by the abolition of all rural sports" and that bulls, when they were in the ascendant in the contest, did not dislike the situation. In 1809, Lord Erskine introduced a bill to protect cattle and horses from malicious wounding, wanton cruelty, and beating, this one opposed by Windham because it would be used against the "lower orders" when the real culprits would be property owners. Judge Edward Abbott Parry writes that the House of Lords found the proposal so sentimental that they drowned Erskine out with cat calls and cock crowing.

1822: Martin's Act

Further information: Badger baiting, Bull baiting, and Cockfighting

> If I had a donkey wot wouldn't go,
> D' ye think I'd wollop him? No, no, no!
> But gentle means I'd try, d' ye see,
> Because I hate all cruelty.
> If all had been like me, in fact,
> There'd ha' been no occasion for Martin's Act.
> — Music hall ditty inspired by the prosecution under Martin's Act of Bill Burns for cruelty to a donkey.

In 1821, the Treatment of Horses bill was introduced by Colonel Richard Martin, MP for Galway in Ireland, but it was lost among laughter in the House of Commons that the next thing would be rights for asses, dogs, and cats.

Nicknamed "Humanity Dick" by George IV, Martin finally succeeded in 1822 with his "Ill Treatment of Horses and Cattle Bill," or "Martin's Act", as it became known, the world's first major piece of animal protection legislation. It was given royal assent on June 22 that year as *An Act to prevent the cruel and improper Treatment of Cattle*, and made it an offence, punishable by fines up to five pounds or two months imprisonment, to "beat, abuse, or ill-treat any horse, mare, gelding, mule, ass, ox, cow, heifer, steer, sheep or other cattle." Any citizen was entitled to bring charges under the Act.

Legge and Brooman argue that the success of the Bill lay in the personality of "Humanity Dick," who was able to shrug off the ridicule from the House of Commons, and whose own sense of humour managed to capture its attention. It was Martin himself who brought the first prosecution under the Act, when he had Bill Burns, a costermonger—a street seller of fruit—arrested for beating a donkey. Seeing in court that the magistrates seemed bored and didn't much care about the donkey, he sent for it, parading its injuries before a reportedly astonished court. Burns was fined, becoming the first person in the world known to have been convicted of animal cruelty. Newspapers and music halls were full of jokes about the "Trial of Bill Burns," as it became known, and how Martin had relied on the testimony of a donkey, giving Martin's Act some welcome publicity. The trial became the subject of a painting (right), which hangs in the headquarters of the RSPCA in London.

The Trial of Bill Burns, showing Richard Martin with the donkey in an astonished courtroom, leading to the world's first known conviction for animal cruelty.

Other countries followed suit in passing legislation or making decisions that favoured animals. In 1822, the courts in New York ruled that wanton cruelty to animals was a misdemeanor at common law. In France in 1850, Jacques Philippe Delmas de Grammont succeeded in having the *Loi Grammont* passed, outlawing cruelty against domestic animals, and leading to years of arguments about whether bulls could be classed as domestic in order to ban bullfighting. The state of Washington followed in 1859, New York in 1866, California in 1868, Florida in 1889. In England, a series of amendments extended the reach of the 1822 Act, which became the Cruelty to Animals Act 1835, outlawing cockfighting, baiting, and dog fighting, followed by another amendment in 1849, and again in 1876.

1824: Society for the Prevention of Cruelty to Animals

> At a meeting of the Society instituted for the purpose of preventing cruelty to animals, on the 16th day of June 1824, at Old Slaughter's Coffee House, St. Martin's Lane: T F Buxton Esqr, MP, in the Chair,
>
> It was resolved:
>
> That a committee be appointed to superintend the Publication of Tracts, Sermons, and similar modes of influencing public opinion, to consist of the following Gentlemen:
>
> Sir Jas. Mackintosh MP, A Warre Esqr. MP, Wm. Wilberforce Esqr. MP, Basil Montagu Esqr., Revd. A Broome, Revd. G Bonner, Revd G A Hatch, A E Kendal Esqr., Lewis Gompertz Esqr., Wm. Mudford Esqr., Dr. Henderson.
>
> Resolved also:
>
> That a Committee be appointed to adopt measures for Inspecting the Markets and Streets of the Metropolis, the Slaughter Houses, the conduct of Coachmen, etc.- etc, consisting of the following Gentlemen:
>
> T F Buxton Esqr. MP, Richard Martin Esqr., MP, Sir James Graham, L B Allen Esqr., C C Wilson Esqr., Jno. Brogden Esqr., Alderman Brydges, A E Kendal Esqr., E Lodge Esqr., J Martin Esqr. T G Meymott Esqr.
>
> A. Broome,
>
> Honorary Secretary

Further information: Royal Society for the Prevention of Cruelty to Animals

Richard Martin soon realized that magistrates did not take the Martin Act seriously, and that it was not being reliably enforced. Several members of parliament decided to form a society to bring prosecutions under the Act. The Reverend Arthur Broome, a Balliol man who had recently become the vicar of Bromley-by-Bow, arranged a meeting in Old Slaughter's Coffee House in St. Martin's Lane, a London café frequented by artists and actors.

The group met on June 16, 1824, and included a number of MPs: Richard Martin, Sir James Mackintosh, Sir Thomas Buxton, William Wilberforce, and Sir James Graham, who had been an MP, and who became one again in 1826. They decided to form a "Society instituted for the purpose of preventing cruelty to animals," or the Society for the Prevention of Cruelty to Animals, as it became known. It determined to send men to inspect the Smithfield Market in the City of London, where livestock had been sold since the 10th century, as well as slaughterhouses, and the practices of coachmen toward their horses. The Society became the Royal Society in 1840, when it was granted a royal charter by Queen Victoria, herself strongly opposed to vivisection.

1824: Early examples of direct action

Noel Molland writes that, in 1824, Catherine Smithies, an anti-slavery activist, set up an SPCA youth wing called the Bands of Mercy. It was a children's club modeled on the Temperance Society's Bands of Hope, which were intended to encourage children to campaign against drinking and gambling. The Bands of Mercy were similarly meant to encourage a love of animals.

Molland writes that some of its members responded with more enthusiasm than Smithies intended, and became known for engaging in direct action against hunters by sabotaging their rifles, although Kim

Stallwood of the Animal Rights Network writes he has often heard these stories but has never been able to find solid evidence to support them. Whether the story is true or apocryphal, the idea of the youth group was revived by Ronnie Lee in 1972, when he and Cliff Goodman set up the Band of Mercy as a militant, anti-hunting guerrilla group, which slashed hunters' vehicles' tires and smashed their windows. In 1976, some of the same activists, sensing that the Band of Mercy name sounded too accommodating, founded the Animal Liberation Front.

1866: American SPCA

The first animal protection group in the United States was the American Society for the Prevention of Cruelty to Animals (ASPCA), founded by Henry Bergh in April 1866. Bergh had been appointed by President Abraham Lincoln to a diplomatic post in Russia, and had been disturbed by the treatment of animals there. He consulted with the president of the RSPCA in London, the Earl of Harrowby, and returned to the U.S. to speak out against bullfights, cockfights, and the beating of horses. He created a "Declaration of the Rights of Animals," and in 1866, persuaded the New York state legislature to pass anti-cruelty legislation and to grant the ASPCA the authority to enforce it.

Other groups

The remainder of the century saw the creation of many animal protection groups. In 1875, the Irish feminist Frances Power Cobbe founded the Society for the Protection of Animals Liable to Vivisection, the world's first organization opposed to animal research, which became the National Anti-Vivisection Society. In 1898, she set up the British Union for the Abolition of Vivisection, with which she campaigned against the use of dogs in research, coming close to success with the 1919 Dogs (Protection) Bill, which almost became law.

1824: Development of the concept of animal rights

The period saw the first extended interest in the idea that non-humans might have natural rights, or ought to have legal ones. In 1824, Lewis Gompertz, one of the men who attended the first meeting of the SPCA in June that year, published *Moral Inquiries on the Situation of Man and of Brutes*, in which he argued that every living creature, human and non-human, has more right to the use of its own body than anyone else has to use it, and that our duty to promote happiness applies equally to all beings.

In 1879, Edward Nicholson argued in *Rights of an Animal* that animals have the same natural right to life and liberty that human beings do, arguing strongly against Descartes' mechanistic view, or what he called the "Neo-Cartesian snake," that they lack consciousness. Other writers of the time who explored whether animals might have natural rights were John Lewis, Edward Evans, and J. Howard Moore.

1839: Schopenhauer

The development in England of the concept of animal rights was strongly supported by the German philosopher, Arthur Schopenhauer (1788–1860). He wrote that Europeans were "awakening more and more to a sense that beasts have rights, in proportion as the strange notion is being gradually overcome and outgrown, that the animal kingdom came into existence solely for the benefit and pleasure of man." He applauded the animal protection movement in England—"To the honor, then, of the English be it said that they are the first people who have, in downright earnest, extended the protecting arm of the law to animals."—and argued against the dominant Kantian idea that animal cruelty is wrong only insofar as it brutalizes humans:

For Schopenhauer, the view that cruelty is wrong only because it hardens human beings was "revolting and abominable."

> Thus only for practice are we to have sympathy for animals, and they are, so to speak, the pathological phantom for the purpose of practicing sympathy for human beings. In common with the whole of Asia not tainted by Islam (that is, Judaism), I regard such propositions as revolting and abominable ... [T]his philosophical morality ... is only a theological one in disguise ... Thus, because Christian morality leaves animals out of account ... they are at once outlawed in philosophical morals; they are mere "things," mere *means* to any ends whatsoever. They can therefore be used for vivisection, hunting, coursing, bullfights, and horse racing, and can be whipped to death as they struggle along with heavy carts of stone. Shame on such a morality that is worthy of pariahs, chandalas, and mlechchhas, and that fails to recognize the eternal essence that exists in every living thing ...

Schopenhauer's views on animal rights stopped short of advocating vegetarianism, arguing that, so long as an animal's death was quick, men would suffer more by not eating meat than animals would suffer by being eaten. He wrote in *The Basis of Morality*: "It is asserted that beasts have no rights ... that 'there are no duties to be fulfilled towards animals.' Such a view is one of revolting coarseness, a barbarism of the West, whose source is Judaism." A few passages later, he called the idea that animals exist for human benefit a "Jewish stence."

1894: Henry Salt and an "epistemological breakthrough"

In 1894, Henry Salt, a former master at Eton, who had set up the Humanitarian League to lobby for a ban on hunting the year before, created what Keith Tester of the University of Portsmouth has called an "epistemological break," in *Animals' Rights: Considered in Relation to Social Progress*. Salt wrote that the object of his essay was to "set the principle of animals' rights on a consistent and intelligible footing, [and] to show that this principle underlies the various efforts of humanitarian reformers ..."

Concessions to the demands for *jus animalium* have been made grudgingly to date, he writes, with an eye on the interests of animals *qua* property, rather than as rights bearers:

> Even the leading advocates of animal rights seem to have shrunk from basing their claim on the only argument which can ultimately be held to be a really sufficient one—the assertion that animals, as well as men, though, of course, to a far less extent than men, are possessed of a distinctive individuality, and, therefore, are in justice entitled to live their lives with a due measure of that "restricted freedom" to which Herbert Spencer alludes.

He argued that there is no point in claiming rights for animals if we subordinate those rights to human desire, and took issue with the idea that the life of a human might have more moral worth or purpose. "[The] notion of the life of an animal having 'no moral purpose,' belongs to a class of ideas which cannot possibly be accepted by the advanced humanitarian thought of the present day—it is a purely arbitrary assumption, at variance with our best instincts, at variance with our best science, and absolutely fatal (if the subject be clearly thought out) to any full realization of animals' rights. If we are ever going to do justice to the lower races, we must get rid of the antiquated notion of a "great gulf" fixed between them and mankind, and must recognize the common bond of humanity that unites all living beings in one universal brotherhood."

Late 1890s: Opposition to anthropomorphism

Further information: Behaviorism and B. F. Skinner

Richard Ryder writes that attitudes toward animals began to harden in the late 1890s, when scientists embraced the idea that what they saw as anthropomorphism—the attribution of human qualities to non-humans—was unscientific. Animals had to be approached as physiological entities only, as Ivan Pavlov wrote in 1927, "without any need to resort to fantastic speculations as to the existence of any possible subjective states." This stance hearkened back to the position of Descartes in the 17th century that non-humans were purely mechanical, like clocks, with no rationality and perhaps even with no consciousness.

20th century: Increase in animal use; animal rights movement

Further information: Animal Welfare Act of 1966, Brown Dog Affair, Animal liberation movement, Animals (Scientific Procedures) Act 1986, and List of animal rights groups

1933: *Tierschutzgesetz*

Further information: Animal protection in Nazi Germany, Animal rights and the Holocaust, Ecofascism, Nazi human experimentation, The Holocaust#Medical experiments, and Vegetarianism of Adolf Hitler

On coming to power in January 1933, the Nazi Party passed the most comprehensive set of animal protection laws in Europe. Kathleen Kete of Trinity College, Hartford, Connecticut writes that it was the first known attempt by a government to break the species barrier, the traditional binary of humans and animals. Humans as a species lost their sacrosanct status, with Aryans at the top of the hierarchy, followed by wolves, eagles, and pigs, and Jews languishing with rats at the bottom. Kete writes that it was the worst possible answer to the question of what our relationship with other species ought to be.

On November 24, 1933, the *Tierschutzgesetz*, or animal protection law, was introduced, with Adolf Hitler announcing an end to animal cruelty: "*Im neuen Reich darf es keine Tierquälerei mehr geben.*" ("In the new Reich, no more animal cruelty will be allowed.") It was followed on July 3, 1934 by the *Reichsjagdgesetz*, prohibiting hunting; on July 1, 1935 by the *Naturschutzgesetz*, a comprehensive piece of environmental legislation; on November 13, 1937 by a law regulating animal transport by car; and on September 8, 1938 by a similar one dealing with animals on trains. The least painful way to shoe a horse was prescribed, as was the correct way to cook a lobster to prevent them from being boiled alive. Several senior Nazis, including Hitler, Rudolf Hess, Joseph Goebbels, and Heinrich Himmler, adopted some form of vegetarianism, though by most accounts not strictly, with Hitler allowing himself the occasional dish of meat. Himmler also mandated vegetarianism for senior SS officers, although this was due mainly to health concerns rather than for animal welfare.

Shortly before the *Tierschutzgesetz* was introduced, vivisection was first banned, then restricted. Animal research was viewed as part of "Jewish science," and "internationalist" medicine, indicating a mechanistic mind that saw nature as something to be dominated, rather than respected. Hermann Göring first announced a ban on August 16, 1933, following Hitler's wishes, but Hitler's personal physician, Dr. Morrel, reportedly persuaded him that this was not in the interests of German research, and in particular defence research. The ban was therefore revised three weeks later, on September 5, 1933, when eight conditions were announced under which animal tests could be conducted, with a view to reducing pain and unnecessary experiments. Primates, horses, dogs, and cats were given special protection, and licenses to conduct vivisection were to be given to institutions, not to individuals. The removal of the ban was justified with the announcement: "It is a law of every community that, when necessary, single individuals are sacrificed in the interests of the entire body."

Medical experiments were later conducted on Jews and Romani children in camps, particularly in Auschwitz by Dr. Josef Mengele, and on others regarded as inferior, including prisoners-of-war. Because the human subjects were often in such poor health, researchers feared that the results of the experiments were unreliable, and so human experiments were repeated on animals. Dr Hans Nachtheim, for example, induced epilepsy on human adults and children without their consent by injecting them with cardiazol, then repeated the experiments on rabbits to check the results.

Post 1945: Increase in animal use

Despite the proliferation of animal protection legislation, animals had no legal rights. Debbie Legge writes that existing legislation was very much tied to the idea of human interests, whether protecting human sensibilities by outlawing cruelty, or protecting property rights by making sure animals were not damaged. The over-exploitation of fishing stocks, for example, is viewed as harming the environment for people; the hunting of animals to extinction means that humans in the future will derive no enjoyment from them; poaching results in financial loss to the owner, and so on.

Notwithstanding the interest in animal welfare of the previous century, the situation for animals arguably deteriorated in the 20th century, particularly after the Second World War. This was in part because of the increase in the numbers used in animal research—300 in the UK in 1875, 19,084 in 1903, and 2.8 million in 2005 (50–100 million worldwide) and an modern annual estimated range of 10 million to upwards of 100 million in the U.S.—but mostly because of the industrialization of farming, which saw billions of animals raised and killed for food each year on a scale not possible before the war.

1960s: Formation of the Oxford group

A small group of intellectuals, particularly at Oxford University—now known as the Oxford Group—began to view the increasing use of animals as unacceptable exploitation. In 1964, Ruth Harrison published *Animal Machines*, a critique of factory farming, which proved influential. Psychologist Richard D. Ryder, who became a member of the Oxford Group, cites a 1965 *Sunday Times* article by novelist Brigid Brophy, called "The Rights of Animals," as having encouraged his own interest. He writes that it was the first time a major newspaper had devoted so much space to the issue. Robert Garner of the University of Leicester writes that Harrison's and Brophy's articles led to an explosion of interest in the relationship between humans and non-humans, or what Garner calls the "new morality."

Brophy wrote:

> The relationship of homo sapiens to the other animals is one of unremitting exploitation. We employ their work; we eat and wear them. We exploit them to serve our superstitions: whereas we used to sacrifice them to our gods and tear out their entrails in order to foresee the future, we now sacrifice them to science, and experiment on their entrail in the hope—or on the mere offchance—that we might thereby see a little more clearly into the present ... To us it seems incredible that the Greek philosophers should have scanned so deeply into right and wrong and yet never noticed the immorality of slavery. Perhaps 3000 years from now it will seem equally incredible that we do not notice the immorality of our own oppression of animals.

Ryder had been disturbed by incidents he had witnessed as a researcher in animal laboratories in the UK and U.S., and in what he calls a "spontaneous eruption of thought and indignation," he wrote letters to the editor of *The Daily Telegraph* about the issue, which were published on April 7, May 3, and May 20, 1969. Brophy read them, and put Ryder in touch with Oxford philosophers Stanley and Roslind Godlovitch, and John Harris, who were working on a book of moral philosophy about the treatment of animals. Ryder subsequently became a contributor to their highly influential *Animals, Men and Morals: An Inquiry into the Maltreatment of Non-humans* (1971), as did Harrison and Brophy. Rosalind Godlovitch's essay "Animal and Morals" was published in the same year.

1970: Coining the term "speciesism"

In 1970, Ryder coined the phrase "speciesism" in a privately printed pamphlet—having first thought of it in the bath—to describe the assignment of value to the interests of beings on the basis of their membership of a particular species. Peter Singer used the term in *Animal Liberation* in 1975, and it stuck within the animal rights movement, becoming an entry in the *Oxford English Dictionary* in 1989.

1975: Publication of *Animal Liberation*

Further information: Animal Liberation (book) and Animal rights#Utilitarian approach

It was in a review of *Animals, Men and Morals* for *The New York Review of Books* on April 5, 1973, that the Australian philosopher, Peter Singer, first put forward his arguments in favour of animal liberation, which have become pivotal within the movement. He based his arguments on the principle of utilitarianism, the view, broadly speaking, that an act is right insofar as it leads to the "greatest happiness of the greatest number," a phrase first used in 1776 by Jeremy Bentham in *A Fragment on Government*. He drew an explicit comparison between the liberation of women and the liberation of animals.

In 1970, over lunch in Oxford with fellow student Richard Keshen, who was a vegetarian, Singer first came to believe that, by eating animals, he was engaging in the oppression of other species by his own. Keshen introduced Singer to the Godlovitches, and Singer and Roslind Godlovitch spent hours together refining their views. Singer's review of the Godlovitches' book evolved into *Animal Liberation*, published in 1975, now widely regarded as the "bible" of the modern animal rights movement.

Although he regards himself as an animal rights advocate, Singer uses the term "right" as "shorthand for the kind of protection that we give to all members of our species." There is no rights theory in his work. He rejects the idea that humans or non-humans have natural or moral rights, and proposes instead the equal consideration of interests, arguing that there are no logical, moral, or biological grounds to suppose that a violation of the basic interests of a human—for example, the interest in not suffering—is different in any morally significant way from a violation of the basic interests of a non-human. Singer's position is that of the English philosopher Henry Sidgwick (1838–1900), who wrote: "The good of any one individual is of no more importance, from the point of view ... of the Universe, than the good of any other."

The publication of *Animal Liberation* triggered a groundswell of scholarly interest in animal rights. Tom Regan wrote in 2001 that philosophers had written more about animal rights in the previous 20 years than in the 2,000 years before that. Robert Garner writes that Charles Magel's extensive bibliography of the literature, *Keyguide to Information Sources in Animal Rights* (1989), contains 10 pages of philosophical material on animals up to 1970, but 13 pages between 1970 and 1989.

1976: Founding of the Animal Liberation Front

Main articles: Animal Liberation Front, Timeline of ALF actions, Anarchism and animal rights, and Veganarchism

In parallel with the Oxford Group, grassroots activists were also developing ideas about animal rights. A British law student, Ronnie Lee, formed an anti-hunting activist group in Luton in 1971, later calling it the Band of Mercy after a 19th-century RSPCA youth group. The Band attacked hunters' vehicles by slashing tires and breaking windows, calling their brand of activism "active compassion." In November 1973, they engaged in their first act of arson when they set fire to a Hoechst Pharmaceuticals research laboratory near Milton Keynes. The Band claimed responsibility, identifying itself to the press as a "nonviolent guerilla organization dedicated to the liberation of animals from all forms of cruelty and persecution at the hands of mankind."

In parallel with the development of the Oxford Group, grassroots activists set up the Animal Liberation Front in 1976.

> The people who run this country, they have shares, they have investments in pharmaceutical companies ... who are experimenting on animals, so to think that you can write to these people, and say "we don't like what you're doing, we want you to change," and expect them to do so, it's not going to happen. — Keith Mann, ALF.

In August 1974, Lee and another activist were sentenced to three years in prison. They were paroled after 12 months, with Lee emerging more militant than ever. In 1976, he brought together the remaining Band of Mercy activists, with some fresh faces, 30 activists in all, in order to start a new movement. He called it the Animal Liberation Front (ALF), a name he hoped would come to "haunt" those who used animals.

The ALF is now active in 38 countries, operating as a leaderless resistance, with covert cells acting on a need to know basis, often learning of each other's existence only when acts of "liberation" are claimed. Activists see themselves as a modern Underground Railroad, the network that helped slaves escape from the U.S. to Canada, passing animals from ALF cells, who have removed them from farms and laboratories, to sympathetic veterinarians to safe houses and finally to sanctuaries. Controversially, some activists also engage in sabotage and arson, as well as threats and intimidation, acts that have lost the movement a great deal of sympathy in mainstream public opinion.

> *My secretary called me to say that I had to contact ... the Metropolitan police ... to receive a fax of a press release that I was going to be murdered if an animal rights activist (Barry Horne on hunger strike) died. ... It's very difficult for [the children] to understand that Daddy goes to work every morning, and, you know, whether he's going to come back.* — Clive Page, professor of pulmonary pharmacology, King's College, London.

The decentralized model of activism is intensely frustrating for law enforcement organizations, who find the cells and networks difficult to infiltrate, because they tend to be organized around known friends. In 2005, the U.S. Department of Homeland Security indicated how seriously it takes the ALF when it included them in a list of domestic terrorist threats.

The tactics of some of the more determined ALF activists are anathema to many animal rights advocates, such as Singer, who regard the animal rights movement as something that should occupy the moral high ground, an impossible claim to sustain when others are bombing buildings and risking lives in the name of the same idea. ALF activists respond to the criticism with the argument that, as Ingrid Newkirk of PETA puts it, "Thinkers may prepare revolutions, but bandits must carry them out."

1980: Henry Spira and "reintegrative shaming"

Henry Spira, a former seaman and civil rights activist, became the most notable of the new animal advocates in the United States. A proponent of gradual change, he introduced the idea of "reintegrative shaming," whereby a relationship is formed between a group of animal rights advocates and a corporation they see as misusing animals, with a view to obtaining concessions or halting a particular practice.

Spira's first campaign was in opposition to the American Museum of Natural History in 1976, where cats were being experimented on, research that he successfully persuaded them to halt. His most notable achievement was in 1980, when he convinced the cosmetics company Revlon to stop using the Draize test, whereby ingredients are dripped into the eyes of rabbits to test for toxicity. He took out a full-page ad in several newspapers, featuring a rabbit with sticking plaster over the eyes, which asked, "How many rabbits does Revlon blind for beauty's sake?" Revlon stopped using animals for cosmetics testing, donated money to help set up Center for Alternatives to Animal Testing, and was swiftly followed by other leading cosmetics companies.

The techniques Spira used have been widely adopted by animal rights groups, most notably by People for the Ethical Treatment of Animals. The approach has its critics on the abolitionist side of the movement, such as Gary Francione, who argue that it aligns the movement with 19th-century animal welfare societies, making them "new welfarists," rather than animal rights groups proper. It takes the movement back to its roots, critics argue, rather than moving toward the paradigm shift that the abolitionists want to see, whereby humans stop seeing animals as property, rather than as property to be treated kindly.

21st century: First rights proposed for animals

January 2008: Court rulings about chimpanzee personhood

In January 2008, Austria's Supreme Court ruled that Matthew Hiasl Pan, a chimpanzee, was not a person, after the Association Against Animal Factories sought personhood status for it because its custodians went bankrupt. Matthew was captured as a baby in Sierra Leone in 1982, then smuggled to Austria to be used in pharmaceutical experiments, but was confiscated by customs officials when it arrived in the country and taken to the shelter instead. It was kept there for 25 years, but the group that ran the shelter went bankrupt in 2007. Donors offered to help it, but under Austrian law only a person can receive personal gifts, so any money sent to Matthew would be lost to the shelter's bankruptcy. The Association has appealed the ruling to the European Court of Human Rights. The lawyer proposing its personhood, Eberhart Theuer, has asked the court to appoint a legal guardian for Matthew and to grant it four rights: the right to life, limited freedom of movement, personal safety, and the right to claim property.

June 2008: Spain passes rights resolution for non-human primates

On June 25, 2008, a committee of Spain's national legislature became the first to vote for a resolution to extend limited rights to non-human primates. The parliamentary Environment Committee recommended giving chimpanzees, bonobos, gorillas, and orangutans the right not to be used in medical experiments or in circuses, and recommended making it illegal to kill apes, except in self-defense, based upon Peter Singer's Great Ape Project (GAP). Pedro Pozas of GAP in Spain called it "a historic day in the struggle for animal rights ... which will doubtless go down in the history of humanity." The committee's proposal has not yet been enacted into law.

January 2010: Dolphin intelligence

In January 2010, a team of scientists announced research results suggesting that dolphins are second in intelligence only to human beings, and that they should be regarded as "non-human persons."

Main philosophical approaches

Overview

Further information: Consequentialism and Deontological ethics

There are two main philosophical approaches to the issue of animal rights: a utilitarian and a rights-based one. The former is exemplified by Peter Singer, professor of bioethics at Princeton University, and the latter by Tom Regan, professor emeritus of philosophy at North Carolina State University, and Gary Francione, professor of law and philosophy at Rutgers School of Law-Newark. Their differences reflect a distinction philosophers draw between ethical theories that judge the rightness of an act by its consequences (called consequentialism, teleological ethics, or utilitarianism, which is Singer's position), and those that judge acts to be right or wrong *in themselves*, almost regardless of consequences (called deontological ethics, of which Regan and Francione are adherents). A consequentialist might argue, for example, that lying is wrong if the lie will make someone unhappy. A deontologist would argue that lying is wrong in principle.

Within the animal rights debate, Singer does not believe there are such things as natural rights and that animals have them, although he uses the language of rights as shorthand for how we ought to treat individuals. Instead, he argues that, when we weigh the consequences of an act in order to judge whether it is right or wrong, the interests of animals, primarily their interest in avoiding suffering, ought to be given equal consideration to the similar interests of humans. That is, where the suffering of one individual, human or non-human, is equivalent to that of any other, there is no moral reason to award more weight to either one of them. Regan's and Francione's approaches are not driven by the weighing of consequences. Regan believes that animals are what he calls "subjects-of-a-life," who have moral rights for that reason, and that moral rights ought not to be ignored. Francione argues that animals have one moral right, and need one legal one: the right not to be regarded as property. All else will follow from that one paradigm shift, he argues.

Utilitarian approach

Further information: Act utilitarianism, Animal language, Animal Liberation (book), and Preference utilitarianism

Peter Singer: Equal consideration of interests

Singer is an act utilitarian, or more specifically a preference utilitarian, meaning that he judges the rightness of an act by its consequences, and specifically by the extent to which it satisfies the preferences of those affected, maximizing pleasure and minimizing pain. (There are other forms of utilitarianism, such as rule utilitarianism, which judges the rightness of an act according to the usual consequences of whichever moral rule the act is an instance of.)

Singer's position is that there are no moral grounds for failing to give equal consideration to the interests of human and non-humans. His principle of equality does not require equal or identical treatment, but equal consideration of interests. A mouse and a man both have an interest in not being kicked down the street, because both would suffer if so kicked, and there are no moral or logical grounds, Singer argues, for failing to accord their interests in not being kicked equal weight. Singer quotes the English philosopher Henry Sidgwick: "The good of any one individual is of no more importance, from the point of view ... of the Universe, than the good of any other." This reflects Jeremy Bentham's position: "[E]ach to count for one, and none for more than one." Unlike the position of a man or a mouse, a stone would not suffer if kicked down the street, and therefore has no interest in avoiding it. Interests, Singer argues, are predicated on the ability to suffer, and nothing more, and once it is established that a being has interests, those interests must be given equal consideration. The issue of the extent to which animals can suffer is therefore key.

Animal suffering

Singer writes that commentators on all sides of the debate now accept that animals suffer and feel pain, although it was not always so. Bernard Rollin, a philosopher and professor of animal sciences, writes that Descartes' influence continued to be felt until the 1980s. Veterinarians trained in the U.S. before 1989 were taught to ignore pain, he writes, and at least one major veterinary hospital in the 1960s did not stock narcotic analgesics for animal pain control. In his interactions with scientists, he was often asked to "prove" that animals are conscious, and to provide "scientifically acceptable" evidence that they could feel pain.

Singer writes that scientific publications have made it clear over the last two decades that the majority of researchers do believe animals suffer and feel pain, though it continues to be argued that their suffering may be reduced by an inability to experience the same dread of anticipation as humans, or to remember the suffering as vividly. In the most recent edition of *Animal Liberation,* Singer cites research indicating that animal impulses, emotions, and feelings are located in the diencephalon, pointing out that this region is well developed in mammals and birds. Singer also relies on the work of Richard Sarjeant to support his position. Sarjeant pointed out that non-human animals possess anatomical complexity of the cerebral cortex and neuroanatomy that is nearly identical to that of the human nervous system, arguing that, "[e]very particle of factual evidence supports the contention that the higher mammalian vertebrates experience pain sensations at least as acute as our own. To say that they feel less because they are lower animals is an absurdity; it can easily be shown that many of their senses are far more acute than ours."

The problem of animal suffering, and animal consciousness in general, arises primarily because animals have no language, leading scientists to argue that it is impossible to know when an animal is suffering. This situation may change as increasing numbers of chimps are taught sign language, although skeptics question whether their use of it portrays real understanding. Singer writes that, following the argument that language is needed to communicate pain, it would often be impossible to know when humans are in pain. All we can do is observe pain behavior, he writes, and make a calculated guess based on it. As Ludwig Wittgenstein argued, if someone is screaming, clutching a part of their body, moaning quietly, or apparently unable to function, especially when followed by an event that we believe would cause pain in ourselves, that is in large measure what it *means* to be in pain. Singer argues that there is no reason to suppose animal pain behavior would have a different meaning.

Equality a prescription, not a fact

> *They talk about this thing in the head; what do they call it?* ["Intellect," whispered someone nearby.] *That's it. What's that got to do with women's rights or Negroes' rights? If my cup won't hold but a pint and yours holds a quart, wouldn't you be mean not to let me have my little half-measure full?* — Sojourner Truth

Singer argues that equality between humans is not based on anything factual, but is simply a prescription. Humans do, in fact, differ in many ways. If the equality of the sexes were based on the idea, for example, that men and women are in principle capable of being equally intelligent, but this was later found to be false, it would mean we would have to abandon the practice of equal consideration. But equality of consideration is based on a prescription, not a description. It is, Singer writes, a moral idea, not an assertion of fact. He quotes President Thomas Jefferson, the principal author in 1776 of the American Declaration of Independence: "Because Sir Isaac Newton was superior to others in understanding, he was not therefore lord of the property or persons of others."

Rights-based approach

Tom Regan: Subjects-of-a-life

Tom Regan argues in *The Case for Animal Rights* and *Empty Cages* that non-human animals are what he calls "subjects-of-a-life," and as such are bearers of rights. He argues that, because the moral rights of humans are based on their possession of certain cognitive abilities, and because these abilities are also possessed by at least some non-human animals, such animals must have the same moral rights as humans. Although only humans act as moral agents, both marginal-case humans, such as infants, and at least some non-humans must have the status of "moral patients." Moral patients are unable to formulate moral principles, and as such are unable to do right or wrong, even though what they do may be beneficial or harmful. Only moral agents are able to engage in moral action.

Animals for Regan have "inherent value" as subjects-of-a-life, and cannot be regarded as a means to an end. This is also called the "direct duty" view. His theory does not extend to all sentient animals but only to those that can be regarded as subjects-of-a-life. He argues that all normal mammals of at least one year of age would qualify in this regard. Whereas Singer is primarily concerned with improving the treatment of animals and accepts that, in some hypothetical scenarios, individual animals might be used legitimately to further human or non-human ends, Regan believes we ought to treat non-human animals as we would humans. He applies the strict Kantian ideal (which Kant himself applied only to humans) that they ought never to be sacrificed as a means to an end, and must be treated as ends in themselves.

Gary Francione: Abolitionism

Abolitionism falls within the framework of the rights-based approach, though it regards only one right as necessary: the right not to be owned. Abolitionists argue that the key to reducing animal suffering is to recognize that legal ownership of sentient beings is unjust and must be abolished. The most prominent of the abolitionists is Gary Francione, professor of law and philosophy at Rutgers School of Law-Newark. He argues that focusing on animal welfare may actually worsen the position of animals, because it entrenches the view of them as property, and makes the public more comfortable about using them.

Francione calls animal rights group who pursue animal welfare issues, such as People for the Ethical Treatment of Animals, the "new welfarists," arguing that they have more in common with 19th-century animal protectionists than with the animal rights movement. He argues that there is no animal rights movement in the United States.

Critics

Carl Cohen

Critics such as Carl Cohen, professor of philosophy at the University of Michigan and the University of Michigan Medical School, oppose the granting of personhood to animals, arguing that rights holders must be able to distinguish between their own interests and what is right. "The holders of rights must have the capacity to comprehend rules of duty governing all, including themselves. In applying such rules, [they] ... must recognize possible conflicts between what is in their own interest and what is just. Only in a community of beings capable of self-restricting moral judgments can the concept of a right be correctly invoked."

Carl Cohen argues that animals cannot distinguish their interests from what is right.

Cohen rejects Singer's argument that, since a brain-damaged human could not make moral judgments, moral judgments cannot be used as the distinguishing characteristic for determining who is awarded rights. Cohen writes that the test for moral judgment "is not a test to be administered to humans one by one," but should be applied to the capacity of members of the species in general.

Posner–Singer debate

Judge Richard Posner of the United States Court of Appeals for the Seventh Circuit debated the issue of animal rights with Peter Singer on *Slate*. Posner argues that his moral intuition tells him "that human beings prefer their own. If a dog threatens a human infant, even if it requires causing more pain to the dog to stop it, than the dog would have caused to the infant, then we favour the child. It would be monstrous to spare the dog."

Singer challenges Posner's moral intuition by arguing that formerly unequal rights for gays, women, and certain races were justified using the same set of intuitions. Posner replies that equality in civil rights did not occur because of ethical arguments, but because facts mounted that there were no morally significant differences between humans based on race, sex, or sexual orientation that would support inequality. If and when similar facts emerge about the difference, or lack thereof, between humans and animals, the differences in rights will erode too. But facts will drive equality, not ethical arguments that run contrary to instinct, he argues.

Posner calls his approach "soft utilitarianism," in contrast to Singer's "hard utilitarianism." He argues: "The "soft" utilitarian position on animal rights is a moral intuition of many, probably most, Americans. We realize that animals feel pain, and we think that to inflict pain without a reason is bad. Nothing of practical value is added by dressing up this intuition in the language of philosophy; much is lost when the intuition is made a stage in a logical argument. When kindness toward animals is levered into a duty of weighting the pains of animals and of people equally, bizarre vistas of social engineering are opened up."

Roger Scruton

> *Considerate la vostra semenza:*
> *Fatti non foste a viver come bruti,*
> *Ma per segue virtute e conoscenza.*
> ("You were not made to live as brutes
> but to follow virtue and knowledge.")
> — Dante, cited by Scruton.

The British philosopher Roger Scruton argues that rights imply obligations. Every legal privilege, he writes, imposes a burden on the one who does not possess that privilege: that is, "your right may be my duty." Scruton therefore regards the emergence of the animal rights movement as "the strangest cultural shift within the liberal worldview," because the idea of rights and responsibilities is, he argues, distinctive to the human condition, and it makes no sense to spread them beyond our own species.

He accuses animal rights advocates of "pre-scientific" anthropomorphism, attributing traits to animals that are, he says, Beatrix Potter-like, where "only man is vile." It is within this fiction that the appeal of animal rights lies, he argues. The world of animals is non-judgmental, filled with dogs who return our affection almost no matter what we do to them, and cats who pretend to be affectionate when, in fact, they care only about themselves. It is, he argues, a fantasy, a world of escape.

See also

- Animal chaplains
- Animal cognition
- Anti-hunting
- Antinaturalism (politics)
- Cruelty to animals
- Deep ecology
- Ethics of eating meat
- Intrinsic value (animal ethics)
- Moral shocks
- Plant rights
- *Striking at the Roots* (book)
- World Animal Day

Further reading

Books and papers

Classic texts

These are the classic animal rights texts according to Robert Garner's *The political theory of animal rights*. Manchester University Press, 2005, p. 9.

- Clark, Stephen R. L. *The Moral Status of Animals*. Oxford University Press, 1977; Clarendon Press, 1984.
- Midgley, Mary. *Animals and Why They Matter*. Penguin Books, 1983; University of Georgia Press, 1998.
- Regan, Tom. *The Case for Animal Rights*. University of California Press, 1983, 1985, 2004.
- Singer, Peter. *Animal Liberation*. HarperCollins, 1975; Cape 1990.

Other

- Adams, Carol J. *The Sexual Politics of Meat: A Feminist-Vegetarian Critical Theory.* [2] New York: Continuum, 1996.
- Adams, Carole. *The Pornography of Meat.* [3] New York: Continuum, 2004.
- Adams, Carole and Josephine, Donovan (eds.). *Animals and Women: Feminist Theoretical Explorations.* [4] London: Duke University Press, 1995.
- *The Social Construction of Edible Bodies and Humans as Predators* [5]
- Adams, Douglas. *Meeting a Gorilla* [6].
- Anstötz, Christopher. *Profoundly Intellectually Disabled Humans* [7]
- Auxter, Thomas. *The Right Not to Be Eaten* [8]

- Barnes, Donald J. *A Matter of Change* [9]
- Barry, Brian. *Why Not Noah's Ark?* [10]
- Bekoff, Marc. *Common Sense, Cognitive Ethology and Evolution* [11].
- Best, Steven. *Terrorists or Freedom Fighters? Reflections on the Liberation of Animals* [12], Lantern Books, 2004. ISBN 1-59056-054-X
- Brent A. Singer. *An Extension of Rawls' Theory of Justice to Environmental Ethics*. Environmental Ethics 10, 1988, p. 217–231
- Cantor, David. *Items of Property* [13].
- Cate, Dexter L. *The Island of the Dragon* [14]
- Cavalieri, Paola. *The Great Ape Project — and Beyond* [15]
- Chapouthier, Georges and Nouët, Jean-Claude (eds), *The universal declaration of animal rights, comments and intentions*, Publisher: Ligue Française des Droits de l'Animal, Paris,1998.
- Clark, Stephen R.L. *The Nature of the Beast*. Oxford University Press 1982; pbk 1984.
- Clark, Stephen R.L. *Animals and their Moral Standing* [16]. Routledge 1997.
- Clark, Stephen R.L. *The Political Animal* [17]. (Routledge 1999)
- Clark, Stephen R.L. *Biology and Christian Ethics* [18]. Cambridge University Press 2000. ISBN 978-0-521-56768-8
- Clark, Ward M. *Misplaced Compassion: The Animal Rights Movement Exposed*, Writer's Club Press, 2001.
- Dawkins, Richard. *Gaps in the mind* [19].
- Dawn, Karen. the Monkey: Rethinking the Way We Treat Animals [20], Harper Collins, 2008
- Dunayer, Joan. "Animal Equality, Language and Liberation". 2001.
- Francione, Gary. *Rain Without Thunder: The Ideology of the Animal Rights Movement*. Temple University Press, 1996.
- Francione, Gary L. *Animals Property & The Law*. Temple University Press, 1995.
- Francione, Gary L. *Introduction to Animal Rights, Your child or the dog?* [21], Philadelphia: Temple University Press, 2000.
- Francione, Gary L. *Animals as Persons: Essays on the Abolition of Animal Exploitation*. Columbia University Press, 2008.
- Favre, David S. *Animal Law: Welfare, Interests, and Rights*, Aspen Law, Stu. Stg. edition, 2008
- Franklin, Julian H. *Animal Rights and Moral Philosophy*, University of Columbia Press, 2005.
- Gruen, Lori. "The Moral Status of Animals" [22], *Stanford Encyclopedia of Philosophy*, July 1, 2003, accessed June 13, 2010.
- Hall, Lee. *Capers in the Churchyard: Animal Rights Advocacy in the Age of Terror*, Nectar Bat Press, 2006
- Hall, Lee. *On Their Own Terms: Bringing Animal-Rights Philosophy Down to Earth*, Nectar Bat Press, 2010

- Kean, Hilda. *Animal Rights: Political and Social Change in Britain since 1800* [23], London: Reaktion Books, 1998
- Mann, Keith, (2007) *From Dusk 'til Dawn: An Insider's View of the Growth of the Animal Liberation Movement*, Puppy Pincher Press, ISBN 978-0-9555850-0-5
- Nibert, David. *Animal Rights, Human Rights: Entanglements of Oppression and Liberation* [24], New York: Rowman and Litterfield, 2002
- Patterson, Charles. *Eternal Treblinka: Our Treatment of Animals and the Holocaust* [25]. New York: Lantern, 2002. ISBN 1-930051-99-9
- Rowlands, Mark. *Animal Rights. A Defense*. New York, London: Macmillan, 1998
- Ryder, Richard. D. *Animal Revolution: Changing Attitudes towards Speciesism* [26], Oxford: Basil Blackwell, 1989
- Scarce, Rik. Eco-Warriors (2006) (ISBN 1-59874-028-8)
- Scruton, Roger. *Animal Rights and Wrongs* [27] Claridge Press, 2000
- Shevelow, Kathryn. *For the Love of Animals: The Rise of the Animal Protection Movement*, Henry Holt and Company, 2008
- Spiegel, Marjorie. *The Dreaded Comparison: Human and Animal Slavery*, New York: Mirror Books, 1996.
- Steeves, H. Peter (ed.) *Animal Others: On Ethics, Ontology, and Animal Life.* [28] New York: SUNY Press, 1999.
- Sztybel, David. "Can the Treatment of Animals Be Compared to the Holocaust?" Ethics and the Environment 11 (Spring 2006): 97–132.
- Sztybel, David. "The Rights of Animal Persons." [29] Animal Liberation Philosophy and Policy Journal 4 (1) (2006): 1–37.
- Taylor, Angus. *Animals and Ethics: An Overview of the Philosophical Debate* [30], 3rd ed., Peterborough: Broadview Press, 2009. ISBN 978-1-55111-976-2
- VanDeVeer, Donald. *Of Beasts, Persons, and the Original Position*. The Monist 62, 1979, p. 368–377
- Weil, Zoe. *The Power and Promise of Humane Education.* [31] British Columbia: New Society Publishers, 2004.
- Wolfe, Cary. *Animal Rites: American Culture, the Discourse of Species, and Posthumanist Theory* [32], Chicago: University of Chicago Press: 2003.
- Wolch, Jennifer, & Emel, Jody. *Animal Geographies: Place, Politics, and Identity in the Nature-Culture Borderlands.* [33] New York: Verso, 1998.

External links

- *Animal Law Review* [34], Lewis & Clark Law School, accessed June 13, 2010.
- Animal Law section [35], The National Association for Biomedical Research, accessed June 13, 2010.
- Animal Legal Defense Fund [36], accessed June 13, 2010.
- Animal rights history [37], animalrightshistory.org, accessed June 13, 2010.
- Regan, Tom. Video of "Animal Rights: An Introduction" [38], Interdisciplinary Lectures on Animal Rights, Ruprecht-Karls-University Heidelberg, May 24, 2006, accessed June 13, 2010.
- The Center on Animal Liberation Affairs [39], accessed June 13, 2010.
- The Tom Regan Animal Rights archive [40], North Carolina State University, accessed June 13, 2010.

Speciesism

Animal liberation

Main articles
Animal rights
Animal liberation movement
Animal law

Issues

Animal Enterprise Terrorism Act
Animal testing
Bile bear • Blood sport
Covance • Draize test
Factory farming • Fur trade
Great Ape research ban • HLS
Lab animal sources • LD50
Meat • Nafovanny • Open rescue
Operation Backfire • Primate trade
Seal hunting • Speciesism • Veganism

Cases
Britches • Brown Dog affair
Cambridge • Pit of despair
Silver Spring monkeys
Unnecessary Fuss

Notable writers
Carol Adams • Jeremy Bentham
Steven Best • Stephen Clark
Gary Francione • Gill Langley
Mary Midgley • Tom Regan
Bernard Rollin • Richard Ryder
Henry Salt • Peter Singer
Steven Wise • Roger Yates

Notable activists
Greg Avery • David Barbarash
Mel Broughton • Rod Coronado
Barry Horne • Ronnie Lee
Keith Mann • Ingrid Newkirk
Heather Nicholson • Jill Phipps
Craig Rosebraugh • Henry Spira
Andrew Tyler • Jerry Vlasak
Paul Watson • Robin Webb

Notable groups/campaigns
List of animal rights groups
Animal Aid • ALDF • ALF • BUAV
GAP • Hunt Saboteurs • PETA • PCRM
Sea Shepherd • SPEAK • SHAC

Political parties
List of animal advocacy parties
Animal Alliance • Animals Count
Animal Protection Party
PACMA
Party for the Animals
Tierschutzpartei

Books and magazines
AR books • AR magazines
Animal Liberation
Arkangel • *Bite Back*
No Compromise

Films
Animal rights films
Behind the Mask • *Earthlings*
The Animals Film
Peaceable Kingdom • *Unnecessary Fuss*

Related categories
ALF • Animal testing
Animal law • Animal rights
AR movement • Blood sports
Livestock • Meat
Poultry

Related templates
Rights • Animal testing
Agriculture • Fishing

Speciesism is the assigning of different values or rights to beings on the basis of their species membership. The term was created by British psychologist Richard D. Ryder in 1973 to denote a prejudice against non-humans based on physical differences that are given moral value however, it can also refer to misanthropy, a hatred of all humans because they are human. "I use the word 'speciesism'," he wrote in 1975, "to describe the widespread discrimination that is practised by man against other species ... Speciesism is discrimination, and like all discrimination it overlooks or underestimates the similarities between the discriminator and those discriminated against."

The term is mostly used by animal rights advocates, who argue that it is irrational or morally wrong to regard sentient beings as objects or property. However, other philosophers and scientists came to defend speciesism as an acceptable if not laudable position.

Philosopher Tom Regan argues that all animals have inherent rights and that we cannot assign them a lesser value because of a perceived lack of rationality, while assigning a higher value to infants and the mentally impaired solely on the grounds of being members of a specific species. Others argue that this valuation of a human infant, a human fetus, or a mentally impaired person is justified, not because the fetus is a fully rational human person from conception, nor because the mentally impaired are rational to the same degree as other human beings; but because the teleological and genetic orientation of any human being from conception is to develop into a rational human being and not any other creature, and because all humans have an implicit origination from two genetically human beings, and hence, both a primary genetic orientation and primary origination as the reproduction of other human beings, even if in a not fully developed state or if partially impaired. In this view, anyone who is born of human parents has the rights of human persons from conception, because the natural process of reproduction has already been initiated in biologically human organisms. Peter Singer's philosophical arguments against speciesism are based on the principle of equal consideration of interests.

Proponents

Some philosophers and scientists defend Speciesism as an acceptable if not good behavior for humans. Carl Cohen, a Professor of Philosophy at the Residential College of the University of Michigan, writes:

> I am a speciesist. Speciesism is not merely plausible; it is essential for right conduct, because those who will not make the morally relevant distinctions among species are almost certain, in consequence, to misapprehend their true obligations.

Jeffrey Alan Gray, British psychologist and a lecturer in experimental psychology at Oxford, similarly wrote that:

> I would guess that the view that human beings matter to other human beings more than animals do is, to say the least, widespread. At any rate, I wish to defend speciesism...

A common theme in defending speciesism tends to be the argument that humans "have the right to compete with and exploit other species to preserve and protect the human species".

Opponents

Gary Francione's position differs significantly from that of Singer, author of *Animal Liberation* (1975). Singer, a utilitarian, rejects moral rights as a general matter and, like Ryder, regards sentience as sufficient for moral status. Singer maintains that most animals do not care about *whether* we kill and use them for our own purposes; they care only about *how* we treat them when we do use and kill them. As a result, and despite our having laws that supposedly protect animals, Francione contends that we treat animals in ways that would be regarded as torture if only humans were involved.

Richard Dawkins touches briefly on the subject in *The Blind Watchmaker* and *The God Delusion*, elucidating the connection to evolutionary theory. He compares former racist attitudes and assumptions to their present-day speciesist counterparts. In a chapter of former book entitled "The one true tree of life", he argues that it is not just zoological taxonomy that is saved from awkward ambiguity by the extinction of intermediate forms, but also human ethics and law. He describes discrimination against chimpanzees thus:

> Such is the breathtaking speciesism of our Christian-inspired attitudes, the abortion of a single human zygote (most of them are destined to be spontaneously aborted anyway) can arouse more moral solicitude and righteous indignation than the vivisection of any number of intelligent adult chimpanzees! [...] The only reason we can be comfortable with such a double standard is that the intermediates between humans and chimps are all dead.

Dawkins more recently elaborated on his personal position towards speciesism and vegetarianism in a live discussion with Singer at The Center for Inquiry on December 7, 2007.

> What I am doing is going along with the fact that I live in a society where meat eating is accepted as the norm, and it requires a level of social courage which I haven't yet produced to break out of that. It's a little bit like the position which many people would have held a couple of hundred years ago over slavery. Where lots of people felt morally uneasy about slavery but went along with it because the whole economy of the South depended upon slavery.

David Nibert seeks to expand the field of sociology "in order to understand how social arrangements create oppressive conditions for both humans and other animals". He compares speciesism to racism and sexism.

Some have suggested that simply to fight speciesism is not enough because intrinsic value of nature can be extended beyond sentient beings, termed the ethic of "libertarian extension". This belief system seeks to apply the principle of individual rights not only to all animals but also objects without a nervous system such as trees, plants and rocks.

Ryder rejects this in writing that "value cannot exist in the absence of consciousness or potential consciousness. Thus, rocks and rivers and houses have no interests and no rights of their own. This does not mean, of course, that they are not of value to us, and to many other painients, including those who need them as habitats and who would suffer without them."

Great ape personhood

Main article: Great Ape personhood

Great Ape personhood is a concept in which the attributes of the Great Apes are deemed to merit recognition of their sentience and personhood within the law, as opposed to mere protection under animal cruelty legislation. This would cover matters such as their own best interest being taken into account in their treatment by people.

Animal holocaust

Main article: Animal rights and the Holocaust

David Sztybel holds that the treatment of animals can be compared to the Holocaust in a valid and meaningful way. In his paper *Can the Treatment of Animals Be Compared to the Holocaust?* using a thirty-nine-point comparison Sztybel asserts that the comparison is not offensive and that it does not overlook important differences, or ignore supposed affinities between the human abuse of fellow animals, and the Nazi abuse of fellow humans. The comparison of animal treatment and the Holocaust came into the public eye with People for the Ethical Treatment of Animals' "Holocaust on your Plate" exhibit. Sztybel equates the racism of the Nazis with the speciesism inherent in eating meat, or using animal by-products, particularly those produced on factory farms. However, even among the supports of the concept of speciesism as a critical tool, such comparisons are not always supported. Y. Michael Barilan writes that speciesism is not the same thing as "Nazi racism" because Nazi racism extolled the abuser and condemned the weaker and the abused. He describes speciesism as the recognition of rights on the basis of group membership rather than solely on the basis of moral considerations.

In fiction

In science fiction and works of fantasy speciesism takes on a role similar to racism, discriminating against other sentients based on a sense of superiority. It varies from humans being superior to non-humans, non-humans being superior to humans, or certain non-humans being superior to other non-humans. Such exists on either a terrestrial, extraterrestrial, extragalactic, or extradimensional plane.

Criticism

Philosophical

A painting of the Trial of Bill Burns, showing Richard Martin with the donkey in an astonished courtroom, leading to the world's first known conviction for animal cruelty, a story that delighted London's newspapers and music halls.

(Rev.) John Tuohey writes that the logic behind charges of speciesism fails to hold up, and that, although it has been popularly appealing, it is philosophically flawed. Tuohey claims that, even though the animal rights movement in the United States has been influential in slowing and in some cases stopping biomedical research involving animals, no one has offered a clear and compelling argument for the equality of species. Nel Noddings has criticized Peter Singer's concept of speciesism for being too simplistic, and failing to take into account the context of species preference as concepts of racism and sexism have taken in to account the context of discrimination against humans. Some people who work for racial or sexual equality have said that comparisons between speciesism and racism or sexism are insulting, for example Peter Staudenmaier writes:

> The central analogy to the civil rights movement and the women's movement is trivializing and ahistorical. Both of those social movements were initiated and driven by members of the dispossessed and excluded groups themselves, not by benevolent men or white people acting on their behalf. Both movements were built precisely around the idea of reclaiming and reasserting a shared humanity in the face of a society that had deprived it and denied it.

> No civil rights activist or feminist ever argued, "We're sentient beings too!" They argued, "We're fully human too!" Animal liberation doctrine, far from extending this humanist impulse, directly undermines it. -Peter Staudenmaier

Some more radical opponents of the idea of speciesism believe that animals exist so that humans may make use of them, be it for food, entertainment or other uses. This special status conveys special rights, such as the right to life, and also unique responsibilities, such as stewardship of the environment.[citation needed]

Carl Cohen argued that racism and sexism are wrong because there are no relevant differences between the sexes or races. Between people and animals however, there are significant differences, and they do not qualify for Kantian personhood, and as such have no rights. Animal rights advocates point out that because many humans do not qualify for Kantian personhood, and yet have rights, this cannot be a morally relevant difference.

Objectivism holds that man as the only being with a conceptual consciousness, as the animal possessing a reasoning faculty and the ability to think, which is the key characteristic setting him apart from other animals, and with his life as the standard of moral value, is the *only* species entitled to rights. "To demand that man defer to the "rights" of other species", it is argued, "is to deprive man himself of the right to life".

Religious

Some believers in human exceptionalism base the concept in the Abrahamic religions, such as the verse in Genesis 1:26 "Then God said, "Let Us make man in Our image, according to Our likeness; and let them rule over the fish of the sea and over the birds of the sky and over the cattle and over all the earth, and over every creeping thing that creeps on the earth." " Animal rights advocates argue that dominion refers to stewardship and does not denote any right to mistreat other animals, which is consistent with the Bible. Buddhism, despite its reputation for respect for animals, explicitly accords humans a higher status in the progression of reincarnation. Animals may be reincarnated as humans, conversely, humans based on his behavior/action can be demoted to the next life to non-human forms; but only humans can reach enlightenment. Similarly in Hinduism, animals are respected, as it is believed that each animal has a role to play. Hindus are therefore vegetarians with a deep respect for Cows. Felipe Fernández-Armesto writes that early hunter-gatherer societies such as the Innu and many animist religions lacked a concept of humanity and placed non-human animals and plants on an equal footing with humans.

Scientific

See also: Animal experimentation

Others take a secular approach, such as pointing to evidence of unusual rapid evolution of the human brain and the emergence of "exceptional" aptitudes. As one commentator put it, "Over the course of human history, we have been successful in cultivating our faculties, shaping our development, and impacting upon the wider world in a deliberate fashion, quite distinct from evolutionary processes. Constance K. Perry asserts that the use of 'non-autonomous' animals instead of humans in risky research can be based on solid moral ground and is not necessarily speciesism.

See also

- Anthropocentrism
- Antinaturalism (politics)
- Biocentrism
- Deep ecology
- Humanism
- Misanthropy
- Veganism

References

- Ryder, Richard D. *Victims of Science: The Use of Animals in Research*. Davis-Poynter, 1975.
- —. "All beings that feel pain deserve human rights: Equality of the species is the logical conclusion of post-Darwin morality." *The Guardian, 6 August 2005.*

Further reading

- Dunayer, Joan. 2004. *Speciesism*. Ryce Publishing: Illinois. ISBN 0-9706475-6-5
- Anti-speciesism [1]
- *Les Cahiers Antispécistes* [2] (in French)

External links

- Discussion between Peter Singer and Richard Dawkins [3]

Animal welfare

Animal welfare is the physical and psychological well-being of non-human animals. The term *animal welfare* can also mean human concern for animal welfare or a position in a debate on animal ethics and animal rights.

Systematic concern for animal welfare can be based on awareness that non-human animals are sentient and that consideration should be given to their well-being, especially when they are used by humans. These concerns can include how animals are killed for food, how they are used for scientific research, how they are kept as pets, and how human activities affect the survival of endangered species.

A four-week-old puppy, found alongside a road after flooding in West Virginia, is fed at an Emergency Animal Rescue Service shelter in the Twin Falls State Park.

An ancient object of concern in some civilizations, animal welfare began to take a larger place in western public policy in 19th-century Britain. Today it is a significant focus of interest or activity in veterinary science, in ethics, and in animal welfare organizations.

There are two forms of criticism of the concept of animal welfare, coming from diametrically opposite positions. One view, dating back centuries, asserts that animals are not consciously aware and hence are unable to experience poor welfare. The other view is based on the animal rights position that animals should not be regarded as property and any use of animals by humans is unacceptable. Some authorities thus treat animal welfare and animal rights as two opposing positions. Accordingly, some animal right proponents argue that the perception of better animal welfare facilitates continued and increased exploitation of animals. Others see the increasing concern for animal welfare as incremental steps towards animal rights.

Definitions

In animal ethics, the term *animal welfare* often means animal welfarism.

In Saunders Comprehensive Veterinary Dictionary, animal welfare is defined as "the avoidance of abuse and exploitation of animals by humans by maintaining appropriate standards of accommodation, feeding and general care, the prevention and treatment of disease and the assurance of freedom from harassment, and unnecessary discomfort and pain."

Donald Broom defines the welfare of an animal as "its state as regards its attempts to cope with its environment. This state includes how much it is having to do to cope, the extent to which it is succeeding in or failing to cope, and its associated feelings." He states that "Welfare will vary over a continuum from very good to very poor and studies of welfare will be most effective if a wide range of measures is used."

Yew-Kwang Ng defines animal welfare in terms of welfare economics: "Welfare biology is the study of living things and their environment with respect to their welfare (defined as net happiness, or enjoyment minus suffering). Despite difficulties of ascertaining and measuring welfare and relevancy to normative issues, welfare biology is a positive science."

Animal welfarism

Animal welfarism, also known simply as *welfarism* or *animal welfare*, is the position that it is morally acceptable for humans to use non-human animals, provided that adverse effects on animal welfare are minimized as far as possible, short of not using the animals at all. An example of welfarist thought is Hugh Fearnley-Whittingstall's meat manifesto.[*citation needed*] Point three of eight is:

> Think about the animals that the meat you eat comes from. Are you at all concerned about how they have been treated? Have they lived well? Have they been fed on safe, appropriate foods? Have they been cared for by someone who respects them and enjoys contact with them? Would you like to be sure of that? Perhaps it's time to find out a bit more about where the meat you eat comes from. Or to buy from a source that reassures you about these points.

Robert Garner describes the welfarist position as the most widely-held in modern society. He states that one of the best attempts to clarify this position is given by Robert Nozick:

> Consider the following (too minimal) position about the treatment of animals. So that we can easily refer to it, let us label this position "utilitarianism for animals, Kantianism for people." It says: (1) maximize the total happiness of all living beings; (2) place stringent side constraints on what one may do to human beings. Human beings may not be used or sacrificed for the benefit of others; animals may be used or sacrificed for the benefit of other people or animals only if those benefits are greater than the loss inflicted.

Welfarism is often contrasted with the animal rights and animal liberation positions, which hold that animals should not be used by humans, and should not be regarded as their property. However, it has been argued that both welfarism and animal liberation only make sense if you assume that animals have "subjective welfare". There is some evidence that the observed difference between human belief in animal welfare and animal rights originates from two distinct attitudes towards animals: (1) attitudes towards suffering; and (2) reverence for animals.

Motivation

Motivations to improve the welfare of animals stems from sympathy and empathy. It can also be based on self-interest. For example, animal producers might improve welfare in order to meet consumer demand for products from high welfare systems. Typically, stronger concern is given to animals that are useful to humans (farm animals, pets etc.) than those that are not (pests, wild animals etc.). The different level of sentience that various species possess, or the perception of such differences, also create a shifting level of concern. Somewhat related to this is size, with larger animals being favored.

There is some evidence to suggest that empathy is an inherited trait. Women have greater concern for animals than men in some societies, possibly the result of it being an evolutionarily beneficial trait in societies where women take care of domesticated animals while men hunt. Interestingly, more women have animal phobias than men. But animal phobias are at least partly genetically determined, and this indicates that attitudes towards animals have a genetic component. Also, children exhibit empathy for animals at a very early age , when external influences cannot be an adequate explanation.

Laws punishing cruelty to animals tend to not just be based on welfare concerns but the belief that such behavior has repercussions toward the treatment of other humans by the animal abusers. Another argument against animal cruelty is based on aesthetics.

External factors that affect people's concern for animal welfare include affluence, education, cultural heritage and religious beliefs. Increased affluence in many regions for the past few decades afforded consumers the disposable income to purchase products from high welfare systems. The adaptation of more economically efficient farming systems in these regions were at the expense of animal welfare and to the financial benefit of consumers, both of which were factors in driving the demand for higher welfare for farm animals.

Interest in animal welfare continues to grow, with increasing attention being paid to it by the media, governmental and non-governmental organizations. The volume of scientific research on animal welfare has also increased significantly.

History, principles, practice

See also: Animal rights#Development of the idea

Systematic concern for the well-being of other animals probably arose in the Indus Valley Civilization as the religious ancestors return in animal form, and that animals must therefore be killed with the respect due to a human. This belief is exemplified in the existing religion, Jainism, and in varieties of other Indian religions. Other religions, specially those with roots in the Abrahamic religions, treat animals as the property of their owners, codifying rules for their care and slaughter intended to limit the distress, pain and fear animals experience under human control.

From the outset in 1822, when British MP Richard Martin shepherded a bill through Parliament offering protection from cruelty to cattle, horses, and sheep (earning himself the nickname *Humanity*

Dick), the welfare approach has had human morality, and humane behaviour, at its central concern. Martin was among the founders of the world's first animal welfare organization, the Society for the Prevention of Cruelty to Animals, or SPCA, in 1824. In 1840, Queen Victoria gave the society her blessing, and it became the RSPCA. The society used members' donations to employ a growing network of inspectors, whose job was to identify abusers, gather evidence, and report them to the authorities.

But significant progress in animal welfare did not take place until the late 20th century. In 1965, the UK government commissioned an investigation - led by Professor Roger Brambell - into the welfare of intensively farmed animals, partly in response to concerns raised in Ruth Harrison's 1964 book, Animal Machines. On the basis of Professor Brambell's report, the UK government set up the Farm Animal Welfare Advisory Committee in 1967, which became the Farm Animal Welfare Council in 1979. The committee's first guidelines recommended that animals require the freedoms to "stand up, lie down, turn around, groom themselves and stretch their limbs". The guidelines have since been elaborated to become known as the Five Freedoms:

- Freedom from thirst and hunger - by ready access to fresh water and a diet to maintain full health and vigour.
- Freedom from discomfort - by providing an appropriate environment including shelter and a comfortable resting area.
- Freedom from pain, injury, and disease - by prevention or rapid diagnosis and treatment.
- Freedom to express normal behavior - by providing sufficient space, proper facilities and company of the animal's own kind.
- Freedom from fear and distress - by ensuring conditions and treatment which avoid mental suffering.

A number of animal welfare organisations are campaigning to achieve a Universal Declaration on Animal Welfare (UDAW) at the United Nations. In principle, the Universal Declaration will call on the United Nations to recognise animals as sentient beings, capable of experiencing pain and suffering, and to recognise that animal welfare is an issue of importance as part of the social development of nations worldwide. The campaign to achieve the UDAW is being co-ordinated by the World Society for the Protection of Animals, with a core working group including Compassion in World Farming, the RSPCA, and the Humane Society International (the international branch of HSUS).

Farm animals

Concern for farm animals is mainly focused on factory farming, where farm animals are raised in confinement at high stocking density. Issues revolve around the limiting of natural behavior in animals (see battery cage, veal and gestation crate), and invasive procedures such as debeaking and mulesing. Other issues include methods of animal slaughter, especially ritual slaughter.

While the killing of animals need not necessarily involve suffering, the general public considers killing an animal an act that reduces its welfare. This leads to concerns with premature slaughtering, such as the chick culling. This applies in a lesser extent to all food animals.

Animal welfare science is an emerging field that seeks to answer questions raised by the use of animals, such as whether hens are frustrated when confined in cages, or whether the psychological well-being of animals in laboratories can be maintained.

Welfare laws

On November 5, 2002, Florida voters passed Amendment 10, an amendment to the Florida Constitution banning the confinement of pregnant pigs in gestation crates. The Amendment passed by a margin of 55% for and 45% against. On November 7, 2006, Arizona voters passed Proposition 204 with 62% support. The measure prohibits the confinement of calves in veal crates and breeding sows in gestation crates. On June 28, 2007, Oregon Governor Ted Kulongoski signed a measure into law prohibiting the confinement of pigs in gestation crates (SB 694, 74th Leg. Assembly, Regular Session). On May 14, 2008, Colorado Governor Bill Ritter signed into law a bill, SB 201, that phases out gestation crates and veal crates.

Germany, Switzerland, Sweden, and Austria have all banned battery cages for egg-laying hens. The entire European Union is phasing out battery cages by 2012.

Laboratory animals

In animal testing, the well-being of individual animals tend to be overridden by the potential benefits their sacrifice can bring to a large number of other animals or people. This utilitarian approach might allow intense suffering to be inflicted on individual animals if the trade-off is considered worthwhile, while a more welfare-based approach would afford all animals the right to a minimum standard of welfare.

Other welfare issues includes the quality of animal sources and housing conditions.

Criticisms

At one time, many people denied that animals could feel anything, and thus the concept of animal welfare was meaningless. For example, many Cartesians were of this opinion. Descartes wrote that animals act "without consciousness", much like a machine.. In addition, there are accounts of Descartes visiting slaughter houses to observe how animals died. Believing that the animals were devoid of sentience, Descartes thought the death throes of animals was akin to "taking apart a spring-driven clock"[citation needed]. In the *Discourse*, published in 1637, Descartes wrote that the ability to reason and use language involves being able to respond in complex ways to all the "contingencies of life", something that animals "clearly cannot do". He argued from this that any sounds animals make do not constitute language, but are simply "automatic responses to external stimuli".

Animal rights advocates, such as Gary L. Francione and Tom Regan, argue that the animal welfare position (advocating for the betterment of the condition of animals, but without abolishing animal use) is inconsistent in logic and ethically unacceptable. However, there are some animal rights groups, such as PETA, which support animal welfare measures in the short term to alleviate animal suffering until all animal use is ended. According to PETA's Ingrid Newkirk in an interview with *Wikinews*, there are two issues in animal welfare and animal rights. "If I only could have one thing, it would be to end suffering," said Newkirk. "If you could take things from animals and kill animals all day long without causing them suffering, then I would take it...Everybody should be able to agree that animals should not suffer if you kill them or steal from them by taking the fur off their backs or take their eggs, whatever. But you shouldn't put them through torture to do that."

Abolitionism (animal rights) holds that focusing on animal welfare not only fails to challenge animal suffering, but may actually prolong it by making the exercise of property rights over animals appear less unattractive. The abolitionists' objective is to secure a moral and legal paradigm shift, whereby animals are no longer regarded as property.

See also

- List of animal welfare groups
- List of animal welfare parties
- Abandoned pets
- Animal fancy
- Animal law
- Animal worship
- Behavioral enrichment
- Blood sport
- Feral cat
- Francis of Assisi
- Hunting
- Intrinsic value (animal ethics)
- Overpopulation in companion animals
- Pain in animals
- Poaching
- Puppy mills
- Whaling
- Zoo

External links

- Animal Welfare Index: JM Welfare Index [1]
- The National Agricultural Law Center [2] Animal Welfare Reading Room [3]
- The United States Agricultural & Food Law and Policy Blog: Animal Welfare [4]
- Humane Education Past, Present, and Future [5] from The State of the Animals II: 2003 [6]
- Farm Animal Welfare: Philosophical Aspects [7] from the Encyclopedia of Animal Science
- The Animal Welfare Science Centre [8]

Intrinsic value (animal ethics)

*This article is about human concern for animals. For rules of conduct between animals and other animal behaviour, see **Ethology**.*

The **intrinsic value** of an animal refers to the value it possesses in its own right, as an end-in-itself, as opposed to its Instrumental value, its value to other animals (including human beings). The phrase (often used synonymously with *inherent value*) has been adopted by animal rights advocates. The Dutch *Animal Health and Welfare Act* referred to it in 1981: "Acknowledgment of the intrinsic value of animals means that animals have value in their own right and as a consequence their interests are no longer automatically subordinate to man's interests." This acknowledgement has stirred a debate on what it entails in the context of animal husbandry, animal breeding, vivisection, animal testing and biotechnology.

History of the moral status of animals (1880–1980)

Moral attitudes towards animals in the west (as expressed in public debate and legislation) has changed considerably over time. Until the 2nd half of the 20th century, the use of animals was regulated by prohibiting those activities that were regarded as offensive to humans (the so-called Offence principle) or at odds with human dignity. These regulations were anthropocentric in character: their objective was to protect the moral feelings and values of human individuals. Other forms of legislation concerning animals sprang from agricultural, economical and veterinary motives.

During the second half of the 20th century, the intensification of cattle breeding and the increased use of laboratory animals provoked fierce debates in which the negative consequences for the animals themselves became an issue. Notably during the 1960's and 1970's, pressure groups started to argue on behalf of the interests of animals kept in laboratories and farms. They expressed their discontent with laws that prohibited deliberate cruelty to animals only insofar as feelings of human individuals were offended or the cruelty involved could be regarded as a defamation on human dignity. They called for new forms of legislation that would protect animals for non-anthropocentric reasons.

In these discussions (the moral relevance of the animal's welfare) two key issues were involved. To begin with, the Harm principle, rather than the Offence principle, should be the moral foundation for the protection of animals. Secondly, as to the scepticism expressed by scientists regarding the presence of consciousness and self-awareness in animals, they should be granted the benefit of the doubt by adopting the so-called *analogy postulate*. Applied ethological research into the behaviour of animals in captivity made it clear that the intensive use of animals had negative effects on the animal's health and well-being. Nevertheless, concern for the well-being of animals had to be purged from anthropomorphism and sentimentalism. This point of view is taken for example in a report by the Dutch Federation of Veterinarians in the EEC (FVE, 1978) concerning welfare-problems among domestic animals. This document states that:

> "although the interests of animals often conflict with the demands of society, society remains responsible for the welfare of the animals involved. Considerations regarding animal welfare ought to be based on veterinary, scientific and ethological norms, but not on sentiment. And although animals do not have fundamental rights, human beings have certain moral obligations towards them."

Intrinsic value and animal ethics (1980–2000)

During the 1970's and 1980's, the criticism regarding the living conditions of farm and laboratory animals became mixed up with other social debates, notably the discussions concerning the protection of the (natural) environment and the ones concerning the development of new breeding techniques. Due to this broadening of the issues, other objections against the use of animals for scientific or economic reasons emerged. The instrumental use of the animals, it was said, is hard to reconcile with their *intrinsic* (or *inherent*) value. In 1981 the Dutch government included the intrinsic value-argument in a statement concerning the protection of animals (CRM, 1981). Now a principle was formulated that allowed for the possibility that, in some cases, the interests of animals might prevail over and above those of science and industry. The interests of the animal involved health and well-being as experienced by the animals themselves, independent from considerations concerning their suitability for human use. It was now claimed that animals have an intrinsic value, that is a *good-of-their-own*, and an interest in their own well-being.

Developments within the field of biotechnology broadened the scope of the debate on the moral status of animals even more. After the controversy concerning the transgenic bull Herman and the lactoferrin project of GenePharming, modern biotechnology has almost become a synonym for genetic engineering. In the debate on bull Herman, concern for the intrinsic value of animals became an issue in its own right. Many felt that there was more to intrinsic value than merely the concern for the animal's welfare. Since then, intrinsic value not only refers to the animal's welfare, but also to the moral attitude society takes towards animals (or nature) as such. For some, this stance means a return to the Offence principle, and therefore not helpful in the struggle against anthropocentrism or anthropomorphism. Others however maintain that recognition of the intrinsic value of animals goes beyond animal welfare, since it respects the animal as "centre of its own being".

Analysis of the term *intrinsic value*

The cause of much confusion in the discussion over intrinsic value in relation to the moral status of animals, is the diversity of meanings and connotations associated with intrinsic value. Broadly speaking there are 4 main positions in this debate defining intrinsic value. One can adhere to a meaning of intrinsic value of animals in a sense that is:

- behaviouristic, as a *morally neutral* value that the animal's *own* (hence *intrinsic*) species-specific behaviour seeks to satisfy. Ethologists like Nikolaas Tinbergen and Gerard Baerends refer in this context to expectancy-values (see also ethology)
- utilitarian, as a *formal* basis to grant animals *specific* rights, based upon the idea of sentience and *interests*, defined by ethological knowledge, and defines corresponding human obligations (see also Peter Singer's ideas about Equal consideration of interests)
- deontological, as respect for the animal's *telos* or striving and consequential *fundamental* rights (see also Tom Regan's ideas about *inherent value* and animal rights)
- attitudinal, as *prima facie* respect for all living beings, regardless of qualities like sentience (see also Reverence for Life and Ethical intuitionism and Moral sense theory)

Of the first, behaviouristic interpretation, one can say (since it is *morally neutral*) that it is useless to ethical theory. Of the fourth, attitudinal or intuitionistic interpretation, one can say that it is indiscriminate of sentience or interests, and could be used for any kind of (natural, cultural or abstract) entity worth protecting (including species, cultures, languages, historical buildings or sites, etc). The core issue in the debate over intrinsic value of animals remains between utilitarianists and deontologists.

See also

- Animal rights
- Animal welfare
- Peter Singer
- Tom Regan
- Anthropocentrism
- Intrinsic value (ethics)
- Harm principle
- Ethology
- Relative deprivation
- Biotechnology
- Vegetarianism
- Vivisection
- Animal law
- Moral status of animals in the ancient world

External links

Intrinsic value & the struggle against anthropocentrism [1]

Abolitionism (animal rights)

Abolitionism within the animal rights movement is the idea that the legal ownership of nonhuman animals is unjust, and that it must be abolished before animal suffering can be substantially reduced. The abolitionist position is that focusing on animal welfare not only fails to challenge animal suffering, but may actually prolong it by making the exercise of property rights over animals appear less unattractive. The abolitionists' objective is to secure a moral and legal paradigm shift, whereby animals are no longer regarded as property.

One of the most important abolitionist writers is Gary Francione, professor of law and philosophy at Rutgers School of Law-Newark. He refers to animal rights groups who pursue welfare concerns, such as People for the Ethical Treatment of Animals, as the "new welfarists," arguing that their intervention risks making the public feel more comfortable about its use of animals, entrenching their property status. Francione's position is that there is, in fact, no animal rights movement in the United States.

See also

- Gary Francione
- Roger Yates
- Animal welfare
- Animal rights

Further reading

- Animal Rights: The Abolitionist Approach [1], Gary Francione's website.
- Dunayer, Joan (2004). *Speciesism*
- Dunayer, Joan (2001). *Animal Equality: Language and Liberation*
- Francione, Gary (2008). *Animals as Persons: Essays on the Abolition of Animal Exploitation*
- Francione, Gary (2000). *Introduction to Animal Rights: Your Child or the Dog?*
- Francione, Gary (1996). *Rain Without Thunder: The Ideology of the Animal Rights Movement*
- Francione, Gary (1995). *Animals, Property, and the Law*
- Torres, Bob (2007). *Making a Killing: The Political Economy of Animal Rights*

Wildlife management

Wildlife management by definition attempts to balance the needs of wildlife with the needs of people using the best available science. Wildlife management can include game keeping, wildlife conservation and pest control. Wildlife management has become an integrated science using disciplines such as mathematics, chemistry, biology, ecology, climatology and geography to gain the best results.

Various species of deer are commonly seen wildlife across the Americas and Eurasia.

Wildlife conservation aims to halt the loss in the earths biodiversity by taking into consideration ecological principles such as carrying capacity, disturbance and succession and environmental conditions such as physical geography, pedology and hydrology with the aim of balancing the needs of wildlife with the needs of people.. Most wildlife biologists are concerned with the preservation and improvement of habitats although reinstatement is increasingly being used. Techniques can include reforestation, pest control, nitrification and denitrification, irrigation, coppicing and hedge laying.

Game keeping is the management or control of wildlife for the wellbeing of game birds may include killing other animals which share the same niche or predators to maintain a high population of the more profitable species, such as pheasants introduced into woodland. In his 1933 book *Game Management*, Aldo Leopold, one of the pioneers of wildlife management as a science, defined it as "the art of making land produce sustained annual crops of wild game for recreational use".

Pest control is the control of real or perceived pests and can be for the benefit of wildlife, farmers, game keepers or safety reasons. In the United States, wildlife management practices are often implemented by a governmental agency to uphold a law, such as the Endangered Species Act of 1973. Many wildlife managers are employed by the U.S. Fish and Wildlife Service and by state governments.

In the United Kingdom, wildlife management undertaken by several organizations including government bodies such as the Forestry Commission, Charities such as the RSPB and The Wildlife Trusts and privately hired gamekeepers and contractors. Legislation has also been passed to protect wildlife such as the Wildlife and Countryside Act 1981. The UK government also give farmers subsidies through the Countryside Stewardship Scheme to improve the conservation value of there farms.

History

The profession of wildlife management was established in the United States in the interwar period (1920s-1930s) by Aldo Leopold and others who sought to transcend the purely restrictive policies of the previous generation of conservationists, such as anti-hunting activist William T. Hornaday. Leopold and his close associate Herbert Stoddard, who had both been trained in scientific forestry, argued that modern science and technology could be used to restore and improve wildlife habitat and thus produce abundant "crops" of ducks, deer, and other valued wild animals.

The institutional foundations of the profession of wildlife management were established in the 1930s, when Leopold was granted the first university professorship in wildlife management (1933, University of Wisconsin, Madison), when Leopold's textbook 'Game Management' was published (1933), when The Wildlife Society was founded, when the Journal of Wildlife Management began publishing, and when the first Cooperative Wildlife Research Units were established. Conservationist planned many projects throughout the 1940s. Some of which included the harvesting of female mammals such as deer to decrease rising populations. Others included waterfowl and wetland research. The Fish and Wildlife Management Act was put in place to urge farmers to plant food for wildlife and to provide cover for them.

Wildlife management grew after World War II with the help of the GI Bill and a postwar boom in recreational hunting. An important step in wildlife management in the United States national parks occurred after several years of public controversy regarding the forced reduction of the elk population in Yellowstone National Park. In 1963, United States Secretary of the Interior Stewart Udall appointed an advisory board to collect scientific data to inform future wildlife management. In a paper known as the Leopold Report, the committee observed that culling programs at other national parks had been ineffective, and recommended active management of Yellowstone's elk population.

Since the tumultuous 1970s, when animal rights activists and environmentalists began to challenge some aspects of wildlife management, the profession has been overshadowed by the rise of conservation biology. Although wildlife managers remain central to the implementation of the ESA and other wildlife conservation policies, Conservation biologists have shifted the focus of conservation away from wildlife management's concern with the protection and restoration of single species and toward the maintenance of ecosystems and biodiversity.

Types of wildlife management

There are two general types of wildlife management:

- **Manipulative management** acts on a population, either changing its numbers by direct means or influencing numbers by the indirect means of altering food supply, habitat, density of predators, or prevalence of disease. This is appropriate when a population is to be harvested, or when it slides to an unacceptably low density or increases to an unacceptably high level. Such densities are inevitably the subjective view of the land owner, and may be disputed by animal welfare interests.
- **Custodial management** is preventive or protective. The aim is to minimize external influences on the population and its habitat. It is appropriate in a national park where one of the stated goals is to protect ecological processes. It is also appropriate for conservation of a threatened species where the threat is of external origin rather than being intrinsic to the system.

Opposition

The control of wildlife through culling and hunting has been criticized by animal rights and animal welfare activists. Critics object to the real or perceived cruelty involved in some forms of wildlife management.

Environmentalists have also opposed hunting where they believe it is unnecessary or will negatively affect biodiversity. Critics of game keeping note that habitat manipulation and predator control are often used to maintain artificially inflated populations of valuable game animals (including introduced exotics) without regard to the ecological integrity of the habitat.

Game keepers in the UK claim it to be necessary for wildlife conservation as the amount of countryside they look after exceeds by a factor of nine the amount in nature reserves and national parks.

Management of hunting seasons

Wildlife management studies, research and lobbying by interest groups help designate times of the year when certain wildlife species can be legally hunted, allowing for surplus animals to be removed. In the United States, hunting season and bag limits are determined by guidelines set by the US Department of Interior, Fish and Wildlife Service (USFWS) for migratory game such as waterfowl and other migratory gamebirds. The hunting season and bag limits for state regulated game species such as deer are usually determined by State game Commissions, which are made up of representatives from various interest groups, wildlife biologists, and researchers.

Open and closed season on Deer in the UK is legislated for in the Deer act 1991 and the Deer Act (Scotland) 1996

Open season

Open season is when wildlife is allowed to be hunted by law and is usually not during the breeding season. Hunters may be restricted by sex, age or class of animal, for instance there may be an open season for any male deer with 4 points or better on at least one side.

Limited entry

Where the number of animals taken is to be tightly controlled, managers may have a type of lottery system called limited. Many apply, few are chosen. These hunts may still have age, sex or class restrictions.

Closed season

Closed season is when wildlife is protected from hunting and is usually during its breeding season. Closed season is enforced by law, any hunting during closed season is punishable by law and termed as illegal hunting or poaching.

Type of weapon used

In the wildlife management one of the conservation strategy is that the weapon used for hunting should be the one that cause the least damage to the individual and that it should be an advanced weapon so that it may not miss the target and may not hit another individual. This is very important if the trophy hunting is the case.

See also

- Age class structure
- Anti-hunting
- CITES (Convention on International Trade in Endangered Species of Wild Fauna and Flora)
- Game Warden
- Goose egg addling
- Hughes v. Oklahoma
- Hunting
- Kleppe v. New Mexico
- Land ethic
- List of politically endorsed exterminations of animals
- Lujan v. Defenders of Wildlife
- North American Game Warden Museum
- Nuisance wildlife management
- Pest control

- Reintroduction
- Remote-controlled animal
- Threshold host density
- Wildlife conservation
- Wildlife Enforcement Monitoring System

Further reading
- Bolen, Eric G., Robinson, William. (2002). *Wildlife Ecology and Management*. Prentice Hall.
- Caughley, G., A.R.E. Sinclair. (1994). *Wildlife Ecology and Management*. Blackwell Scientific Publ.

Movements and Groups for Animal Rights

Veganarchism

Veganarchy symbol; popularised by Brian A. Dominick's *Animal Liberation and Social Revolution* pamphlet in 1995. The front cover combined the 'V' from vegan with the anarchist 'A' symbol.

Part of the Politics series on

Anarchism

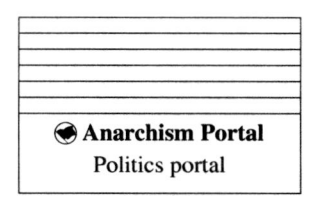

Veganarchism or **vegan anarchism**, is the political philosophy of veganism (more specifically animal liberation and earth liberation) and anarchism, creating a combined praxis that's designed to be a means for social revolution. This encompasses viewing the state as unnecessary and harmful to animals, both human and non-human, whilst practising a vegan lifestyle. It is either perceived as a combined theory, or that both philosophies are essentially the same. It is further described as an anti-speciesist perspective on green anarchism, or an anarchist perspective on animal liberation.

Veganarchists typically view oppressive dynamics within society to be interconnected, from statism, racism and sexism to human supremacy and redefine veganism as a radical philosophy that sees the state as harmful to animals. Ideologically, it is a *human, animal, and Earth liberation* movement that is fought as part of the same struggle.[*citation needed*] Those who believe in veganarchy can be either against reform for animals or for it, although do not limit goals to changes within the law.

The philosophy was first popularised by Brian A. Dominick in *Animal Liberation and Social Revolution* and later promoted by anarcho-punk band *Virus* using symbolism, Roots of Compassion, a zine named 'veganarchy', and political prisoner Jonny Albewhite. The ideology is sometimes referred to as **radical veganism**, **total liberation**, **total revolution**, or **total abolition**, however not all who believe in the terms perceive them to be veganarchy.

Terms

Further information: Anarchist terminology and Anarchist schools of thought

- **Anarchism** is a political philosophy encompassing theories and attitudes which consider the state, as compulsory government, to be unnecessary, harmful, and/or undesirable.
- **Veganism** is a diet and lifestyle that seeks to exclude the exploitation and cruelty to animals for any purposes, endeavoring not to use or consume animal products of any kind.
- **Veganarchists**; those who believe in veganarchism, typically pronounced as *v-ganarchism* to correctly pronounce veganism, and to distinguish the ideology from veg-anarchism and anarchists.
- **Veganarchy** is the goal and aim of proponents of the political philosophy of veganarchism.

Origins

Main articles: Anarchism and animal rights, Green anarchism, and Abolitionism (animal rights)

The term was popularised in 1995 with Brian A. Dominick's pamphlet *Animal Liberation and Social Revolution*, described as *"a vegan perspective on anarchism or an anarchist perspective on veganism"*. It was originally published by *Critical Mess Media*, then in 1997 re-printed by *Firestarter Press* and re-distributed for anti-copyright usage. In 2002 it was translated into Portuguese by *Discórdia edições* and into German by *Autonome Tierbefreiungsaktion Hannover* in 2005, further circulating the essay abroad. It is currently sold by; *AK Press, Active Distribution, Re-pressed Distribution* and *Kids in Misery*.

The 18-page pamphlet explains how many young anarchists in the 1990s had been adopting deep ecological (animal-inclusive and anti-speciesist) mindsets as part of an overall green-anarchist political philosophy. Similarly animal liberationists were becoming increasingly influenced by anarchist thought and traditions, thus becoming veganarchists and adopting an overall praxis.

Brian Dominick described his reasons for the necessity of veganarchism in the opening chapter *The Veganarchists*:

> In this essay I wish to demonstrate that any approach to social change must be comprised of an understanding not only of social relationships, but also between the relationships between humans and nature, including non-human animals. I also hope to show herein why no approach to animal liberation is feasible without a thorough understanding of and immersion in the *social* revolutionary endeavor. We must all become, if you will, "veganarchists".

Issues

Oppression

> *To decide one oppression is valid and the other not is to consciously limit one's understanding of the world; it is to engage oneself in voluntary ignorance, more often than not for personal convenience.* - Brian A. Dominick

In *Animal Liberation and Social Revolution*, Brian A. Dominick describes how he believes relationships between oppressive dynamics within the establishment are interconnected, including; classism, economic oppression, statism, sexism, homophobia, patriarchy, racism (founded within ethnocentrism), ageism, and the result of human supremacy; speciesism and environmental destruction. He claims that throughout history the state has been dependent on these interdependent oppressions. It is further understood that the fate of all species are intricately interrelated, so the exploitation of animals must play a major role on the impact of the human world. This includes the domestication of animals as being partly responsible for the *"emergence of patriarchy, state power, slavery, hierarchy and domination of all kinds"*.[citation needed]

Radicalism

On radical veganism, Dominick defines what veganism means, concluding that to not consume the products of non-human animals is not the true meaning of the term, but one of its lifestyle choices; differentiating it from pure vegetarianism. He criticises self-proclaimed vegans who justify care free consumption of corporate products, citing poor workers conditions and treatment of human labor, comparing them to non-human suffering. Dominick therefore defines veganism as a radical understanding of what human and non-human animal oppression really is, therefore determining lifestyle choices by an informed and politicized opinion.

Reformism

Dominick describes veganarchists as either opposed to reformist measures for animals (considering them the task of liberals or progressives), such as granting non-humans suffrage, or include but do not limit their goals to changes within the law. He criticises the need for the state to *stand between* humans and non-humans, detailing increased crime and violence due to alcohol prohibition and the war on drugs, believing a government orchestrated *"War on Meat"* would only cause more problems rather than curb animal abuse and the reinforced desires for animal products; preferring instead a non-coercive approach to eliminating animal consumption.

Reformist organisations such as HSUS and PETA have come under heavy criticism from anarcho-vegans, who commonly see them as being connected to welfarism, compromise and fundraising for animals, therefore moving away from substantive and meaningful goals. [*citation needed*]

Violence

In *Violence in Everyday Life*, Brian A. Dominick labels society as being largely based on violence, enhanced by corporate control media images. Dominick depicts power as a social concept and that *"those on the receiving end of violence naturally suffer a severe amount of disempowerment"*, usually asserting what little remaining power they have left. He affirms that victims often internalize oppression, carrying it with them, hence becoming victimizers. Further discussing violence, Dominick regards the abuse of animals - whether directly, as with the mistreatment of pets, or indirectly by eating meat, as correlating to social violence.

Direct action

Main articles: Animal liberation movement, Leaderless resistance, Timeline of ALF actions, and Timeline of ELF actions

Some veganarchists engage in direct action. Organizing themselves through groups like Food Not Bombs, Stop Huntingdon Animal Cruelty (SHAC), the Animal Liberation Front (ALF) and Earth Liberation Front (ELF), in autonomous, covert cells, they may take action against the meat and dairy industries, animal testing laboratories, fur farms, logging industries and, more rarely, government institutions.

The ALF acronym within the anarchist symbol 'A'

Such actions are normally, though not always, non-violent. Though not necessarily veganarchists, activists have used the names Animal Rights Militia (ARM), Revolutionary Cells – Animal Liberation Brigade (RCALB), Justice Department, and others to claim responsibility for openly politically violent, heroic attacks.

External links

- On Veganarchism [1], *Indymedia UK*
- Veganarchy.net [2]
    - Veganarchy: Issue 1 [3]
- Veganarchist [4], *Blogspot*
- The Veganarchist [5], *Bravehost*
- The Veganarchist's Vent [6], *Zoomshare*
- Thomas Paine's Corner [7], *Total liberation / anarcho-veganism*
- Question Everything [8], *A Veganarchist Blog with particular focus on Unity of Struggle.*

Animal liberation movement

For the concept, see Animal rights. For other uses, see Animal liberation (disambiguation).

The **animal liberation movement**, sometimes called the **animal rights movement, animal personhood**, or **animal advocacy movement**, is a global movement with roughly three components: philosophical debate, legal development, and direct action. The movement seeks an end to the rigid moral and legal distinction drawn between human and non-human beings, an end to the status of animals as property, and an end to their use in the research, food, clothing, and entertainment industries.

It is one of the few examples of a social movement that was created, and is to a large extent sustained academically, by philosophers.

Terms

All animal liberationists believe that the individual interests of non-human animals deserve recognition and protection, but the movement can be split into two broad camps.

Animal rights advocates, or rights liberationists, believe that these basic interests confer moral rights of some kind on the animals, and/or ought to confer legal rights on them; see, for example, the work of Tom Regan. Utilitarian liberationists, on the other hand, do not believe that animals possess moral rights, but argue, on utilitarian grounds — utilitarianism in its simplest form advocating that we base moral decisions on the greatest happiness of the greatest number — that, because animals have the ability to suffer, their suffering must be taken into account in any moral philosophy. To exclude animals from that consideration, they argue, is a form of discrimination that they call speciesism; see, for example, the work of Peter Singer.

Despite these differences, the terms "animal liberation" and "animal rights" are generally used interchangeably.

History

Further information: 20th century: Increase in animal use; animal rights movement, Gary Francione, Tom Regan, Richard D. Ryder, and Peter Singer

The movement is regarded as having been founded in the UK in the early 1970s by a group of Oxford academics, now known as the "Oxford Group." Psychologist Richard Ryder, who was part of the group, writes that "rarely has a cause been so rationally argued and so intellectually well armed." He cites a 1965 article by novelist Brigid Brophy in the *Sunday Times* as pivotal in helping to spark the movement. Brophy wrote:

Philosopher Peter Singer

> The relationship of homo sapiens to the other animals is one of unremitting exploitation. We employ their work; we eat and wear them. We exploit them to serve our superstitions: whereas we used to sacrifice them to our gods and tear out their entrails in order to foresee the future, we now sacrifice them to science, and experiment on their entrail in the hope — or on the mere offchance — that we might thereby see a little more clearly into the present.

Ryder wrote three letters to the Daily Telegraph in response to Brophy's arguments. Brophy read Ryder's letters and put him in touch with Oxford philosophers Stanley and Roslind Godlovitch, and John Harris, who were working on a book about the issue.

In 1970, Ryder coined the phrase "speciesism," first using it in a privately printed pamphlet to describe the assignment of value to the interests of beings on the basis of their membership of a particular species. Ryder subsequently became a contributor to *Animals, Men and Morals: An Inquiry into the Maltreatment of Non-humans*(1972), edited by John Harris and the Godlovitches, a work that became highly influential, as did Rosalind Godlovitch's essay "Animal and Morals," published the same year.

It was in a review of *Animals, Men and Morals* for the *New York Review of Books* that Australian philosopher Peter Singer first put forward his basic arguments, based on utilitarianism and drawing an explicit comparison between women's liberation and animal liberation. Out of the review came Singer's *Animal Liberation*, published in 1975, now regarded as the "bible" of the movement.

Other books regarded as important include philosopher Tom Regan's *The Case for Animal Rights* (1983); *Created from Animals: The Moral Implications of Darwinism* by James Rachels (1990); *Animals, Property, and the Law* (1995) by legal scholar Gary Francione, *Rattling the Cage: Toward*

Legal Rights for Animals by another legal scholar Steven M. Wise (2000); and *Animal Rights and Moral Philosophy* by Julian H. Franklin (2005).

Nature of the movement

Status

The movement is no longer viewed as hovering on the fringe. In the 1980s and 1990s, it was joined by a wide variety of academics and professionals, including lawyers, physicians, psychologists, veterinarians, and former vivisectionists, and is now a common subject of study in philosophy departments in Europe and North America. Animal law courses are taught in 92 out of 180 law schools in the U.S., and the movement has gained the support of senior legal scholars, including Alan Dershowitz and Laurence Tribe of Harvard Law School. Chapters of animal rights law have been created in several state bar associations, and resolutions related to animal rights are regularly proposed within the American Bar Association.

Michael Socarras of Greenberg Traurig told the Association of American Medical Colleges: "There is a very important shift under way in the manner in which many people in law schools and in the legal profession think about animals. This shift has not yet reached popular opinion. However, in [the U.S.], social change has and can occur through the courts, which in many instances do not operate as democratic institutions. Therefore, the evolution in elite legal opinion is extremely significant ..."

Advocacy

Veganism and vegetarianism

Further information: Factory farming, Live export, Veganism, Vegetarianism, and Veganarchism

Animal liberationists usually boycott industries that use animals. Foremost among these is factory farming, which produces the majority of meat, dairy products, and eggs in industrialized nations. The transportation of farm animals for slaughter, which often involves their live export, has in recent years been a major issue for animal rights groups, particularly in the UK and Scandinavia.

The vast majority of animal rights advocates adopt vegetarian or vegan diets. They may also avoid clothes made of animal skins, such as leather shoes, and will not use products known to contain animal byproducts. Goods containing ingredients that have been tested on animals are also avoided where possible. Company-wide boycotts are common. The Procter & Gamble corporation, for example, tests many of its products on animals, leading many animal rights advocates to boycott the company's products entirely, whether tested on animals or not.

There is a growing trend in the American movement towards devoting all resources to vegetarian outreach. The 9.8 billion animals killed there for food every year far exceeds the number of animals used in other ways. Groups such as Vegan Outreach and Compassion Over Killing devote their time to exposing factory-farming practices by publishing information for consumers and by organizing undercover investigations.

Veganarchism

Main articles: Veganarchism, Anarchism and animal rights, and Green anarchism

Veganarchism is the political philosophy of veganism (more specifically animal liberation) and anarchism, creating a combined praxis as a means for social revolution. This encompasses viewing the state as unnecessary and harmful to animals, both human and non-human, whilst practising a vegan diet. Veganarchists either see the ideology as a combined theory, or perceive both philosophies to be essentially the same. It is further described as an anti-speciesist perspective on green anarchism, or an anarchist perspective on animal liberation.

Veganarchy symbol; combining the 'V' from vegan with the anarchist 'A' symbol.

The term was popularised in 1995 with Brian A. Dominick's pamphlet *Animal Liberation and Social Revolution*, described as *"a vegan perspective on anarchism or an anarchist perspective on veganism"*. The 18-page pamphlet explains how many young anarchists in the 1990s had been adopting deep ecological (animal-inclusive and anti-speciesist) mindsets as part of an overall green anarchist political philosophy. Similarly animal liberationists were becoming increasingly influenced by anarchist thought and traditions, thus becoming veganarchists and adopting an overall praxis.

Direct action

Further information: Animal Liberation Front, SPEAK campaign, Stop Huntingdon Animal Cruelty, List of animal rights groups, Leaderless resistance, and Anarchism and animal rights

Timeline of ALF actions: 1976-1999, 2000-2004 and 2005-Present

The movement espouses a number of approaches, and is bitterly divided on the issue of direct action and violence, with very few activists or writers publicly advocating the latter tactic as a justified method to use. Most groups reject violence against persons, intimidation, threats, and the destruction of property: for example, the British Union for the Abolition of Vivisection (BUAV) and Animal Aid. These groups concentrate on education and research, including carrying out undercover investigations of animal-testing facilities. There is some evidence of cooperation between the BUAV and the ALF: for example, the BUAV used to donate office space for the use of the ALF in London in the early 1980s.

A fire, claimed by the Oxford Arson Squad, caused £500,000 damage to Londbridges boathouse, Oxfordshire on July 4, 2005.

Other groups do not condemn the destruction of property, or intimidation, but do not themselves engage in those activities, concentrating instead on education, research, media campaigns, and undercover investigations: for example, People for the Ethical Treatment of Animals (PETA).

A third category of activists operates using the leaderless resistance model, working in covert cells consisting of small numbers of trusted friends, or of one individual acting alone. These cells engage in direct action: for example by carrying out raids to release animals from laboratories and farms, using names like the Animal Liberation Front (ALF); or by boycotting and targeting anyone or any business associated with the controversial animal testing lab, Huntingdon Life Sciences (HLS), using a campaign name like Stop Huntingdon Animal Cruelty (SHAC).

Activists who have carried out or threatened acts of physical violence have operated using the names; Hunt Retribution Squad (HRS), Animal Rights Militia (ARM), Justice Department and the Revolutionary Cells--Animal Liberation brigade (RCALB).

A November 13, 2003 edition of CBS News' 60 Minutes charged that "eco-terrorists," a term used by the United States government to refer to the Animal Liberation Front and Earth Liberation Front, are considered by the FBI to be "the country's biggest domestic terrorist threat." John Lewis, a Deputy Assistant Director for Counterterrorism at the FBI, stated in a 60 Minutes interview that these groups "have caused over $100 million worth of damage nationwide", and that "there are more than 150 investigations of eco-terrorist crimes underway". In September 2006, the U.S. Senate unanimously passed the "Animal Enterprise Terrorism Act", legislation which would allow federal authorities to "help prevent, better investigate, and prosecute individuals who seek to halt biomedical research through acts of intimidation, harassment, and violence." Many of the ideas used by those who engage in direct action were developed by British activists.

Some activists have attempted blackmail and other illegal activities, such as the intimidation campaign to close Darley Oaks farm, which involved hate mail, malicious phonecalls, hoax bombs, arson attacks and property destruction, climaxing in the theft of the corpse of Gladys Hammond, the owners' mother-in-law, from a Staffordshire grave. Over a thousand ALF attacks in one year in the UK alone caused £2.6M of damage to property, prompting some experts to state that animal rights now tops the list of causes that prompt violence in the UK.

There are also a growing number of "open rescues," in which liberationists enter businesses to remove animals without trying to hide their identities. Open rescues tend to be carried out by committed individuals willing to go to jail if prosecuted, but so far no farmer has been willing to press charges.

Philosophical and legal aims

Further information: Main animal rights philosophical approaches and Veganarchism

The movement aims to include animals in the moral community by putting the basic interests of non-human animals on an equal footing with the basic interests of human beings. A basic interest would be, for example, not being made to suffer pain on behalf of other individual human or non-human animals. The aim is to remove animals from the sphere of property and to award them personhood; that is, to see them awarded legal rights to protect their basic interests.

> Who are we that we have set ourselves up on this pedestal and we believe that we have a right to take from others everything—including their life—simply because we want to do it? Shouldn't we stop and think for a second that maybe they are just others like us? Other nations, other individuals, other cultures. Just others. Not sub-human, but just different from being human.

Liberationists argue that animals appear to have value in law only in relation to their usefulness or benefit to their owners, and are awarded no intrinsic value whatsoever. In the United States, for example, state and federal laws formulate the rules for the treatment of animals in terms of their status as property. Liberationists point out that Texas Animal Cruelty Laws apply only to pets living under the custody of human beings and exclude birds, deer, rabbits, squirrels, and other wild animals not owned by humans, ignoring that juridiction for such creatures comes under the domain of state wildlife officers. The U.S. Animal Welfare Act excludes "pet stores ... state and country fairs, livestock shows, rodeos, purebred dog and cat shows, and any fairs or exhibitions intended to advance agricultural arts and sciences." There is no mention in the law that such activities already fall under the jurisdiction of state agriculture departments. The Department of Agriculture interprets the Act as also excluding cold-blooded animals, and warm-blooded animals not "used for research, teaching, testing, experimentation ... exhibition purposes, or as a pet, [and] farm animals used for food, fiber, or production purposes".

Regarding the campaign to change the status of animals as property, the movement has seen success in several countries. Switzerland passed legislation in 1992 recognizing non-human animals as beings, not things. The German Civil Code had been amended correspondingly two years earlier. In 2002, the words "and animals" were added to the constitutional clause obliging the German state to protect the "natural living conditions", which has been regarded as a milestone in the development of the legal status of animals in Germany. The amendment, however, has not had much impact in German legal practice yet. The greatest success has certainly been the granting of basic rights to five great ape species in New Zealand in 1999. Their use is now forbidden in research, testing or teaching.

The Seattle-based Great Ape Project (GAP) — founded by Australian philosopher Peter Singer, the author of *Animal Liberation*, widely regarded as the founding philosophical work of the animal liberation movement — is campaigning for the United Nations to adopt its Declaration on Great Apes, which would see chimpanzees, bonobos, gorillas and orang-utans included in a "community of equals" with human beings. The declaration wants to extend to the non-human apes the protection of three basic interests: the right to life, the protection of individual liberty, and the prohibition of torture. . The New Zealand success is partly ascribed to GAP´s activity.

Public support

Animal liberation

Main articles
Animal rights
Animal liberation movement
Animal law

Issues

Animal Enterprise Terrorism Act
Animal testing
Bile bear • Blood sport
Covance • Draize test
Factory farming • Fur trade
Great Ape research ban • HLS
Lab animal sources • LD50
Meat • Nafovanny • Open rescue
Operation Backfire • Primate trade
Seal hunting • Speciesism • Veganism

Cases
Britches • Brown Dog affair
Cambridge • Pit of despair
Silver Spring monkeys
Unnecessary Fuss

Notable writers
Carol Adams • Jeremy Bentham
Steven Best • Stephen Clark
Gary Francione • Gill Langley
Mary Midgley • Tom Regan
Bernard Rollin • Richard Ryder
Henry Salt • Peter Singer
Steven Wise • Roger Yates

Notable activists
Greg Avery • David Barbarash
Mel Broughton • Rod Coronado
Barry Horne • Ronnie Lee
Keith Mann • Ingrid Newkirk
Heather Nicholson • Jill Phipps
Craig Rosebraugh • Henry Spira
Andrew Tyler • Jerry Vlasak
Paul Watson • Robin Webb

Notable groups/campaigns
List of animal rights groups
Animal Aid • ALDF • ALF • BUAV
GAP • Hunt Saboteurs • PETA • PCRM
Sea Shepherd • SPEAK • SHAC

Political parties
List of animal advocacy parties
Animal Alliance • Animals Count
Animal Protection Party
PACMA
Party for the Animals
Tierschutzpartei

Books and magazines
AR books • AR magazines
Animal Liberation
Arkangel • *Bite Back*
No Compromise

Films
Animal rights films
Behind the Mask • *Earthlings*
The Animals Film
Peaceable Kingdom • *Unnecessary Fuss*

Related categories
ALF • Animal testing
Animal law • Animal rights
AR movement • Blood sports
Livestock • Meat
Poultry

Related templates
Rights • Animal testing
Agriculture • Fishing

Animal People, an independent newspaper covering the international animal-protection and animal-rights movements, indicates that these issues are increasing in popularity with the public. Citing U.S. IRS (tax) form 990 numbers for 2004, the newspaper says that donations to animal rights groups increased by 40 percent from 2003 to 2004. For example:

- The Humane Society of the United States (animal protection): revenues of $74 million, up 3 percent.
- The Massachusetts Society for Prevention of Cruelty to Animals (animal protection): revenues of $48.2 million, up an 11 percent.
- People for the Ethical Treatment of Animals (animal rights): $28.1 million, up 20 percent.
- Physicians Committee for Responsible Medicine (animal rights): $16 million, up from $12 million.

Animal People estimates the combined budgets of animal protection organizations at more than $290 million in 2004, up from $207 million in 2003.

Terrorism

The U.S. Justice Department labels underground groups the Animal Liberation Front and the Earth Liberation Front as terrorist organizations. Some arson, property destruction and vandalism has been linked to various animal rights groups

Further reading

Articles

- "A Critique of the Kantian Theory of Indirect Moral Duties to Animals" [1] by Jeff Sebo, *AnimalLiberationFront.com*, undated, retrieved September 4, 2005
- "Burning Rage" [2] by Ed Bradley, CBS *60 Minutes*, November 5, 2005
- "FBI, ATF address domestic terrorism" [3], by Terry Frieden, CNN, May 19, 2005
- Animal Liberation Through Trade Unions? [4], No Compromise, Issue 15, 1999
- Movement Watch [5], *Friends of Animals*, 2003

Books

- Keith Mann, *From Dusk 'Til Dawn: An Insiders View of the Growth of the Animal Liberation Movement* [6] (Puppy Pincher Press 2007). ISBN 978-0-9555850-0-5
- Ingrid Newkirk, *Free the Animals: The Story of the Animal Liberation Front*, Lantern Books, 2000). ISBN 1-930051-22-0
- Peter Singer, *Ethics into Action: Henry Spira and the Animal Rights Movement* (Lanham, MD: Bowman & Littlefield, 1998). ISBN 0-8476-9073-3
- Lawrence Finsen and Susan Finsen, *The Animal Rights Movement in America: From Compassion to Respect* (New York: Twayne Publishers, 1994). ISBN 0-8057-3884-3
- Gary L. Francione, *Rain without Thunder: The Ideology of the Animal Rights Movement* (Philadelphia: Temple University Press, 1996). ISBN 1-56639-461-9
- Harold D. Guither, *Animal Rights: History and Scope of a Radical Social Movement* (Carbondale: Southern Illinois University Press, 1998). ISBN 0-8093-2199-8
- James M. Jasper and Dorothy Nelkin, *The Animal Rights Crusade: The Growth of a Moral Protest* (New York: The Free Press, 1992). ISBN 0-02-916195-9

People for the Ethical Treatment of Animals

Founders	Ingrid Newkirk and Alex Pacheco
Type	501(c)(3)
Founded	March 1980
Location	Norfolk, Virginia
Focus	Animal rights
Revenue	$34 million in 2009
Employees	300
Members	2,000,000
Motto	"Animals are not ours to eat, wear, experiment on, or use for entertainment."
Website	www.peta.org [1]

People for the Ethical Treatment of Animals (**PETA**) is an American animal rights organization based in Norfolk, Virginia, and led by Ingrid Newkirk, its international president. A non-profit corporation with 300 employees and two million members and supporters, it says it is the largest animal rights group in the world. Its slogan is "animals are not ours to eat, wear, experiment on, or use for entertainment."

Founded in March 1980 by Newkirk and animal rights activist Alex Pacheco, the organization first caught the public's attention in the summer of 1981 during what became known as the Silver Spring monkeys case, a widely publicized dispute about experiments conducted on 17 macaque monkeys inside the Institute of Behavioral Research in Silver Spring, Maryland. The case lasted ten years, involved the only police raid on an animal laboratory in the United States, triggered an amendment in 1985 to that country's Animal Welfare Act, and established PETA as an internationally known organization. Since then, in its campaigns and undercover investigations, it has focused on four core issues—opposition to factory farming, fur farming, animal testing, and animals in entertainment—though it also campaigns against fishing, the killing of animals regarded as pests, the keeping of chained backyard dogs, cock fighting, dog fighting, and bullfighting.

The group has been the focus of criticism from inside and outside the animal rights movement. Newkirk and Pacheco are seen as the leading exporters of animal rights to the more traditional animal protection groups in the United States, but sections of the movement nevertheless say PETA is not radical enough—law professor Gary Francione calls them the new welfarists, arguing that their work with industries to achieve reform makes them an animal welfare, not an animal rights, group. Newkirk told *Salon* in 2001 that PETA works toward the ideal, but tries in the meantime to provide carrot-and-stick incentives. There has also been criticism from feminists within the movement about the use of scantily clad women in PETA's anti-fur campaigns, and criticism in general that the group's media stunts trivialize animal rights. Newkirk's view is that PETA has a duty to be "press sluts".

Outside the movement, the confrontational nature of PETA's campaigns has caused concern, as has the number of animals it euthanizes. It was further criticized in 2005 by United States Senator Jim Inhofe for having given grants several years earlier to Animal Liberation Front (ALF) and Earth Liberation Front (ELF) activists. PETA responded that it has no involvement in ALF or ELF actions and does not support violence, though Newkirk has elsewhere made clear that she does support the removal of animals from laboratories and other facilities, including as a result of illegal direct action.

History

Ingrid Newkirk

Main article: Ingrid Newkirk

Newkirk was born in England in 1949 and raised in Hertfordshire, and later New Delhi, India, where her father—a navigational engineer—was stationed. Newkirk, now an atheist, was educated in a convent, the only British girl there. She moved to the United States as a teenager, first studying to become a stockbroker, but after taking some abandoned kittens to a shelter in 1969, and appalled by the conditions she found there, she choose a career in animal protection instead. She became an animal protection officer for Montgomery County, then the District of Columbia's first woman poundmaster. By 1976 she was head of the animal-disease-control division of D.C.'s Commission on Public Health, and in 1980 was among those named as Washingtonian of the Year. She told Michael Specter of *The New Yorker* that working for the shelters left her shocked at the way the animals were treated:

> I went to the front office all the time, and I would say, "John is kicking the dogs and putting them into freezers." Or I would say, "They are stepping on the animals, crushing them like grapes, and they don't care." In the end, I would go to work early, before anyone got there, and I would just kill the animals myself. Because I couldn't stand to let them go through that. I must have killed a thousand of them, sometimes dozens every day. Some of those people would take pleasure in making them suffer. Driving home every night, I would cry just thinking about it. And I just felt, to my bones, this cannot be right.

In 1980, she divorced Steve Newkirk, whom she had married when she was 19, and the same year met Alex Pacheco, a political major at George Washington University. Pacheco had studied for the priesthood, then worked as a crew member of the Sea Shepherd Conservation Society's first ship. He volunteered at the shelter where she worked, and they fell in love and began living together, though as Kathy Snow Guillermo writes they were very different—Newkirk was older and more practical, whereas Pacheco could barely look after himself. He introduced Newkirk to Peter Singer's influential book, *Animal Liberation* (1975), and in March 1980 she persuaded him to join her in forming People for the Ethical Treatment of Animals, at that point just five people in a basement, as Newkirk described it. They were mostly students and members of the local vegetarian society, but the group included a friend of Pacheco's from the UK, Kim Stallwood, a British activist who went on to become the national organizer of the British Union for the Abolition of Vivisection . Pacheco was reluctant at first. "It just didn't sound great to me," he told *The Los Angeles Times* in 1992." I had been active in Europe ... and I thought there were just too many formalities. I thought we should just do things ourselves. But she made a convincing case that Washington needed a vehicle for animals because the current organizations were too conservative."

Silver Spring monkeys

Main article: Silver Spring monkeys

The group first came to public attention in 1981 during the Silver Spring monkeys case, a dispute about experiments conducted by researcher Edward Taub on 17 macaque monkeys inside the Institute of Behavioral Research in Silver Spring, Maryland. The case led to the first police raid in the United States on an animal laboratory, triggered an amendment in 1985 to the United States Animal Welfare Act, and became the first animal-testing case to be appealed to the United States Supreme Court, which upheld a Louisiana State Court ruling that denied PETA's request for custody of the monkeys.

Pacheco had taken a job in May 1981 inside a primate research laboratory at the Institute, intending to gain firsthand experience of working inside an animal laboratory. Taub had been cutting sensory ganglia that supplied nerves to the monkeys' fingers, hands, arms, and legs—a process called "deafferentation"—so that the monkeys could not feel them; some of the monkeys had had their entire spinal columns deafferented. He then used restraint, electric shock, and withholding of food and water to force the monkeys to use the deafferented parts of their bodies. The research led in part to the discovery of neuroplasticity and a new therapy for stroke victims called constraint-induced movement therapy.

Pacheco visited the laboratory at night, taking photographs that showed the monkeys living in what the Institute for Laboratory Animal Research's *ILAR Journal* called filthy conditions. He passed his evidence to the police, who raided the lab and arrested Taub. Taub was convicted of six counts of animal cruelty, the first such conviction in the United States of an animal researcher, overturned on appeal. Norm Phelps writes that the case followed the highly publicized campaign of Henry Spira in 1976 against experiments on cats being performed at the American Museum of Natural History in New York, and Spira's subsequent campaign in April 1980 against the Draize test. These and the Silver Springs monkey case jointly put animal rights on the agenda in the United States.

The ten-year battle for custody of the monkeys—described by *The Washington Post* as a vicious mud fight, during which both sides accused the other of lies and distortion— transformed PETA into a national, then international, movement. By February 1991, it claimed over 350,000 members, a paid staff of over 100, and an annual budget of over $7 million.

Philosophy and activism

Profile

Further information: Animal rights

PETA writes that it is an animal rights organization, and as such it rejects speciesism and the idea of animals as property, and opposes the use of animals in any form: as food, clothing, entertainment, or as research subjects. One oft-cited quote of Newkirk's is: "When it comes to feelings like hunger, pain, and thirst, a rat is a pig is a dog is a boy." The group has been criticized by other animal rights advocates for its willingness to work with industries that use animals—a position many animal rights advocates find problematic (see below). Newkirk rejects the criticism, and has said of the group that it is here to hold the radical line.

PETA lobbies governments to impose fines where animal-welfare legislation has been violated, promotes a vegan diet, tries to reform the practices in factory farms and slaughterhouses, goes undercover into animal research laboratories, farms, and circuses, initiates media campaigns against particular companies or practices, helps to find sanctuaries for former circus and zoo animals, and initiates lawsuits against companies.

The group has two million members and supporters, it received donations of over $32 million for the year ending July 31, 2009, and its website was receiving four million hits a month as of November 2008. Over 80 percent of its operating budget was spent on its programs in 2008-2009, 15 percent on fundraising, and four percent on management and general operations. Thirty-two percent of its staff earned under $30,000, 24 percent over $40,000, and Newkirk just under $37,000.

Pacheco left the group in 1999, and since then the two key staff members next to Newkirk have been Bruce Friedrich, director of vegan outreach—a devout Catholic who spent years working in soup kitchens, and who gives 20 percent of his income to the church—and Dan Mathews, the group's senior vice-president.

Campaigns and consumer boycotts

The organization is known for its aggressive media campaigns, combined with a solid base of celebrity support—Pamela Anderson, Drew Barrymore, Alec Baldwin, John Gielgud, Bill Maher, Stella McCartney, and Alicia Silverstone have all appeared in PETA ads. Every week, Newkirk holds what *The New Yorker* calls a war council, with two dozen of her top strategists gathered round a square table in the PETA conference room, no suggestion considered too outrageous. PETA also gives a yearly prize, called the Proggy Award (for "progress"), to individuals or organizations dedicated to animal welfare or who distinguish themselves through their efforts within the area of animal welfare.

Many of the campaigns have focused on large corporations. Fast food companies such as KFC, Wendy's, and Burger King have been targeted. In the animal-testing industry, PETA's consumer boycotts have focused on Avon, Benetton, Bristol-Myers-Squibb, Chesebrough-Pond's, Dow Chemical, General Motors, and others. Their *modus operandi* includes buying shares in target companies such as McDonald's and Kraft Foods in order to exert influence. The campaigns have delivered results for PETA. McDonald's and Wendy's introduced vegetarian options after PETA targeted them; Petco stopped selling some exotic pets; and Polo Ralph Lauren said it would no longer use fur. Avon, Estee Lauder, Benetton, and Tonka Toy Co. all stopped testing products on animals, the Pentagon stopped shooting pigs and goats in wounds tests, and a slaughterhouse in Texas was closed down.

As part of its anti-fur action, PETA members have infiltrated hundreds of fashion shows in the U.S, Europe, and once in China, throwing red paint on the catwalks, and unfurling banners. Celebrities and supermodels have posed naked for the group's "I'd Rather Go Naked than Wear Fur" campaign—some men, but mostly women—triggering criticism from feminist animal rights advocates (see below). *The New Yorker* writes that PETA activists have crawled through the streets of Paris wearing leg-hold traps and thrown around money soaked in fake blood at the International Fur Fair. They regularly engage in pie-throwing—in January 2010, Canadian MP Gerry Byrne compared them to terrorists for throwing a tofu cream pie at Canada's fishery minister Gail Shea in protest at the seal hunt, a comment Newkirk called a silly chest-beating exercise. "The thing is, we make them gawk," she told *Satya* magazine, "maybe like a traffic accident that you have to look at."

Some campaigns have been particularly controversial. Newkirk was criticized in 2003 for sending a letter to PLO leader Yasser Arafat asking him to keep animals out of the conflict, after a donkey was blown up during an attack in Jerusalem. The group's 2003 "Holocaust on your Plate" exhibition—eight 60-square-foot (5.6 m^2) panels juxtaposing images of Holocaust victims with animal carcasses and animals being transported to slaughter—was criticized by the Anti-Defamation League. In July 2010, the German Federal Constitutional Court ruled that PETA's campaign was not protected by free speech laws, and banned it within Germany as an offense against human dignity. In 2005, the NAACP complained about the "Are Animals the New Slaves?" exhibit, which showed images of African-American slaves, Native Americans, child laborers, and women, alongside chained elephants and slaughtered cows.

PETA's "It's still going on" campaign features newspaper ads comparing widely-publicized murder-cannibalization cases to the deaths of animals in slaughterhouses. The campaign has attracted significant media attention, controversy and generated angry responses from the victims' family members. Ads were released in 1991 describing the deaths of the victims of serial killer Jeffrey Dahmer, in 2002 describing the deaths of the victims of serial killer Robert William Pickton, and in 2008 describing the murder of Tim McLean. In several cases, newspapers have refused to run the ads.

The group has also been criticized for aiming its message at young people. "Your Mommy Kills Animals" features a cartoon of a woman attacking a rabbit with a knife. To reduce milk consumption, it created the "Got Beer?" campaign, a parody of the dairy industry's series of Got Milk? ads, which featured celebrities with milk "mustaches" on their upper lips. When the mayor of New York, Rudolf Giuliani, was diagnosed with prostate cancer in 2000, PETA ran a photograph of him with a white mustache and the words "Got prostate cancer?" to illustrate their claim that dairy products contribute to cancer, an ad that caused an outcry in the United States. After PETA placed ads in school newspapers linking milk to acne, obesity, heart disease, cancer, and strokes, Mothers Against Drunk Driving and college officials complained it encouraged underage drinking; the British Advertising Standards Authority asked that the ads be discontinued after complaints from interest groups such as The National Farmers' Unions.

PETA has been criticized for aiming its message at children.

Other campaigns are less confrontational and more humorous. In 2008, it launched the "Save the Sea Kittens" campaign to change the name of fish to "sea kittens" to give them a positive image, and it regularly asks towns to adopt a new name. It campaigned in 1996 for a new name for Fishkill, New York, and in April 2003 offered free veggie burgers to Hamburg, New York, if it would call itself Veggieburg.

Undercover investigations

PETA sends its staff undercover into research laboratories, factory farms, and circuses to document the treatment of animals, requiring them to spend many months as employees of the facility, making copies of documents and wearing hidden cameras. By 2007, it had conducted 75 such investigations. It has also produced videos based on material collected during ALF raids. Some investigations have led to lawsuits or government action against the companies or universities. PETA itself faced legal action in April 2007 after the owners of a chinchilla ranch in Michigan complained about an undercover inquiry there, but the judge ruled in PETA's favor that undercover investigations can be legitimate.

Notable cases include the 26-minute film PETA produced in 1984, *Unnecessary Fuss*, based on 60 hours of researchers' footage obtained by the ALF during a raid on the University of Pennsylvania's head injury clinic. The footage showed researchers laughing at baboons as they inflicted brain damage on them with a hydraulic device intended to simulate whiplash. Laboratory animal veterinarian Larry Carbone writes that the researchers openly discussed how one baboon was awake before the head injury, despite protocols being in place for anaesthesia. The ensuing publicity led to the suspension of funds from the university, the firing of its chief veterinarian, the closure of the lab, and a period of probation for the university.

In 1990, Bobby Berosini, a Las Vegas entertainer, lost his wildlife license, as well as a later lawsuit against PETA, after the group broadcast an undercover film of him slapping and punching orangutans in 1989. In 1997, a PETA investigation inside Huntingdon Life Sciences (HLS), a contract animal-testing company, produced film of staff in the UK beating dogs, and what appeared to be abuse of monkeys in the company's New Jersey facility. After the video footage aired on British television in 1999, a group of activists set up Stop Huntingdon Animal Cruelty to close HLS down, a campaign that continues.

In 1999, a North Carolina grand jury handed down indictments against pig-farm workers on Belcross Farm in Camden County, the first indictments for animal cruelty on a factory farm in the United States, after a three-month PETA investigation produced film of the workers beating the animals. In 2004, PETA published the results of an eight-month undercover investigation in a West Virginia Pilgrim's Pride slaughterhouse that supplies chickens to KFC. *The New York Times* reported the investigation as showing workers stomping on live chickens, throwing dozens against a wall, tearing the head off a chicken to write graffiti, strangling one with a latex glove, and squeezing birds until they exploded. Yum Brands, owner of KFC, called the video appalling, and threatened to stop purchasing from Pilgrim's Pride if no changes were made; Pilgrim's Pride fired 11 employees, and introduced an anti-cruelty pledge for workers to sign.

In 2004 and 2005, PETA shot footage inside Covance, an animal-testing company in the United States and Europe, that appeared to show monkeys being mistreated in the company's facility in Vienna, Virginia. According to *The Washington Post*, PETA said an employee of the group filmed primates there being choked, hit, and denied medical attention when badly injured. After PETA sent the video and a 253-page complaint to the United States Department of Agriculture, Covance was fined $8,720 for 16 citations, three of which involved lab monkeys; the other citations involved administrative issues and equipment. The company said none of the issues were pervasive or endemic, and that they had taken corrective action. In 2005 Covance initiated a lawsuit charging PETA with fraud, violation of employee contract, and conspiracy to harm the company's business, but did not proceed with it.

PETA also goes undercover into circuses. In 2006, they filmed trainers at Carson & Barnes Circus—including Tim Frisco, the animal-care director—striking elephants while shouting at them; *The Washington Post* writes that the video shows Frisco shouting "Make 'em scream!" A company spokesman dismissed PETA's concerns as 'Utopian philosophical ideology," but said the circus would no longer use electric prods.

Positions

On direct action and the ALF

Further information: Animal Liberation Front

Newkirk is outspoken in her support of direct action, writing that no movement for social change has ever succeeded without what she calls the militarism component: "Thinkers may prepare revolutions," she wrote of the ALF in 2004, "but bandits must carry them out."

> Not until black demonstrators resorted to violence did the national government work seriously for civil rights legislation ... In 1850 white abolitionists, having given up on peaceful means, began to encourage and engage in actions that disrupted plantation operations and liberated slaves. Was that all wrong?
> —Ingrid Newkirk, 2004

In 2004 *The Observer* described what it called a network of relationships between apparently unconnected animal rights groups on both sides of the Atlantic, writing that, with assets of $6.5 million, and with the PETA Foundation holding further assets of $15 million, PETA funds a number of activists and groups—some with links to militant groups, including the ALF, which the FBI has named as a domestic terrorist threat. American writer Don Liddick writes that PETA gave $1,500 to the Earth Liberation Front in 2001—Newkirk said the donation was a mistake, and that the money had been intended for public education about destruction of habitat, but Liddick writes that it went to the legal defense of Craig Rosebraugh, an ELF spokesman. That same year, according to *The Observer*, PETA gave a $5,000 grant to American animal rights activist Josh Harper, an advocate of arson.

According to Liddick, PETA has substantial links with Native American ALF activist Rod Coronado. He alleges that two Federal Express packages were sent to an address in Bethesda, Maryland, before and after a 1992 fire at Michigan State University that Coronado was convicted of setting, reportedly as part of "Operation Bite Back," a series of ALF attacks on American animal testing facilities in the 1990s. The first package was picked up by a PETA employee, Maria Blanton, and the second intercepted by the authorities, who identified the handwriting as Coronado's. Liddick writes that the package contained documents removed from the university and a videotape of one of the perpetrators. When they searched Blanton's home, police found some of the paraphernalia of animal liberation raids, including code names for Coronado and Alex Pacheco—PETA's co-founder—burglary tools, two-way radios, and fake identification. Liddick also writes that PETA gave Coronado $45,000 for his legal bills and another $25,000 to his father.

Newkirk is a strong supporter of direct action that removes animals from laboratories and other facilities—she told *The Los Angeles Times* in 1992 that when she hears of anyone walking into a lab and walking out with animals, her heart sings. In an interview for *Wikinews* in 2007, she said she had been asked by other animal protection groups to condemn illegal acts. "And I won't do it, because it were my animal I'd be happy." But she added that she does not support arson. "I would rather that these buildings weren't standing, and so I think at some level I understand. I just don't like the idea of that, but maybe that's wishy-washy of me, because I don't want those buildings standing if they hurt anyone ... Why would you preserve [a building] just so someone can make a profit by continuing to hurt and kill individuals who feel every bit as much as we do?"

On neutering, backyard dogs, working animals, and pets

PETA runs several programs though its Community Animal Project that helps cats and dogs in poorer areas of Virginia, near its headquarters. In 2008 they neutered 7,485 cats, dogs, and rabbits in that area, including pit bulls and feral cats, at a discounted rate or free of charge. They help neglected dogs and cats who are ill and injured, and pursue cruelty cases. Each year they set up hundreds of dog houses with straw bedding for dogs chained outside all winter. They urge population control through neutering and adoption from shelters, and campaign against organizations such as the American Kennel Club that promote the breeding of purebred strains.

PETA argues that it would have been better for animals had the institution of breeding them as "pets" never emerged, that the desire to own and receive love from animals is selfish, and that their breeding, sale, and purchase can cause immeasurable suffering. They write that millions of dogs spend their lives chained outside in all weather conditions or locked up in chain-link pens and wire cages in puppy mills, and that even in good homes animals are often not well cared for. They would like to see the population of dogs and cats reduced through spaying and neutering, and for people never to purchase animals from pet shops or breeders, but to adopt them from shelters instead. PETA is also against the use of animals to assist the blind or disabled as guide dogs or hearing dogs, as well as the use of animals in all roles of work including search and rescue. They argue instead that humans should be relied upon for the support of the disabled.

On euthanasia

Further information: Animal euthanasia

PETA opposes the no kill movement. The group takes in feral cat colonies with diseases such as feline AIDS and leukemia, stray dogs, litters of parvo-infected puppies, and backyard dogs, and says that it would be unrealistic to follow a no-kill policy in such instances. They offer free euthanasia services to counties that kill unwanted animals via gassing or shooting—they recommend the use of an intravenous injection of sodium pentobarbital if administered by a trained professional, and for severely ill or dying pets when euthanasia at a veterinarian is unaffordable. They recommend euthanasia for certain breeds, such as pit bull terriers, and in certain situations for animals in shelters: for example, for those living for long periods in cramped cages.

Two PETA employees were acquitted in 2007 of animal cruelty, but convicted of littering, after at least 80 euthanized animals were left in dumpsters in a shopping center in Ashoskie over the course of a month in 2005; the two employees were seen leaving behind 18 dead animals, and 13 more were found inside their van. The animals had been euthanized after being removed from shelters in Northampton and Bertie counties. The group said it began euthanizing animals in some rural North Carolina shelters after it found the shelters killing animals in ways PETA considered inhumane.

On wildlife conservation personalities

PETA is critical of television personalities they call self-professed wildlife warriors, arguing that while a conservationist message is getting across, some of the actions are harmful to animals, such as invading animals' homes, netting them, subjecting them to stressful environments, and wrestling with them—often involving young animals the group says should be with their mothers. In 2006 when Steve Irwin died, PETA's vice-president Dan Mathews said Irwin had made a career out of antagonizing frightened wild animals. Australian Member of Parliament Bruce Scott said PETA should apologize to Irwin's family and the rest of Australia.

On animal testing

Further information: Animal testing

PETA opposes animal testing—whether toxicity testing, basic or applied research, or for education and training—on both moral and practical grounds. Newkirk told *Vogue* magazine in 1989 that even if it resulted in a cure for AIDS, PETA would oppose it. The group also believes that it is wasteful, unreliable, and irrelevant to human health, because artificially induced diseases in animals are not identical to human diseases. They say that animal experiments are frequently redundant and lack accountability, oversight, and regulation. They promote alternatives, including embryonic stem cell research and in vitro cell research. PETA employees have themselves volunteered for human testing of vaccines; Scott Van Valkenburg, the group's Director of Major Gifts, said in 1999 that he had volunteered for human testing of HIV vaccines.

Position within the animal rights movement

Further information: Animal rights movement

Robert Garner of the University of Leicester writes that Newkirk and Pacheco are the leading exporters of animal rights to the more moderate groups in the United States—both members of an animal rights elite that he argues has shaken up the animal rights movement, setting up new groups and radicalizing old ones.

There is criticism of PETA from both the conservative and radical ends of the movement. Michael Specter writes that it provides for groups such as the Humane Society of the United States the same dynamic that Malcolm X provided for Martin Luther King, or Andrea Dworkin for Gloria

Steinem—someone radical to alienate the mainstream and make moderate voices more appealing. The failure to condemn the Animal Liberation Front triggers complaints from the conservatives, while the more radical activists say the group has lost touch with its grassroots, is soft on the idea of animal rights, and that it should stop the media stunts, the pie-throwing, and the targeting of women. "It's hard enough trying to get people to take animal rights seriously without PETA out there acting like a bunch of jerks," one activist told writer Norm Phelps.

The ads featuring barely clad or naked women have appalled feminist animal rights advocates. When Ronald Reagan's daughter Patti Davis posed naked for *Playboy*, donating half her $100,000 fee to PETA, the group issued a press release saying Davis "turns the other cheek in an eye-opening spread," then announced she had been photographed naked with Hugh Hefner's dog for an anti-fur ad. In 1995, PETA formed a partnership with *Playboy* to promote human organ donation, with the caption "Some People Need You Inside Them" on a photograph of Hefner's wife. The long-standing campaign, "I'd rather go naked than wear fur," in which celebrities and supermodels strip for the camera, generated particular concern.

Newkirk has replied to the criticism that no one is being exploited, the women taking part are volunteers, and if sexual attraction advances the cause of animals, she is unapologetic. Asked by Wikinews how she feels when criticized from within the movement, she said: "Somebody has to push the envelope. If you say something that someone already agrees with, then what's the point, and so we make some more conservative animal protection organizations uncomfortable; they don't want to be associated with us because it will be embarrassing for them, and I understand that. Our own members write to us sometimes and say, 'Oh why did you do this? I don't want anyone to know I'm a PETA member.'"

> If anybody wonders 'what's this with all these reforms?', you can hear us clearly. Our goal is total animal liberation, and the day when everyone believes that animals are not ours to eat, not ours to wear, not ours to experiment [on], and not ours for entertainment or any other exploitive purpose.
> —Ingrid Newkirk, 2002

Gary Francione, professor of law at Rutgers School of Law-Newark, argues that PETA is not an animal rights group—and further that there is no animal rights movement in the United States—because of their willingness to work with industries that use animals to achieve incremental change. This makes them an animal welfare group, in Francione's view: what he calls the new welfarists. A proponent of abolitionism, Francione argues that PETA is trivializing the movement with what he calls the "Three Stooges" theory of animal rights, making the public think progress is underway when the changes are only cosmetic.

Like Francione, PETA describes itself as abolitionist. Newkirk told an animal rights conference in 2002 that PETA's goal remains animal liberation: "Reforms move a society very importantly from A to B, from B to C, from C to D. It's very hard to take a nation or a world that is built on seeing animals as nothing more than hamburgers, handbags, cheap burglar alarms, tools for research, and move them from A to Z ..."

Francione has also criticized PETA for having caused grassroots animal rights group to close, groups that he argues were essential for the survival of the animal rights movement, which rejects the centrality of corporate animal charities. Francione writes that PETA initially set up independent chapters around the United States, but closed them in favor of a top-down, centralized organization, which not only consolidated decision-making power, but centralized donations too. Now, local animal rights donations go to PETA, rather than to a local group.

See also

- Kentucky Fried Cruelty
- People for the Ethical Treatment of Animals v. Doughney
- PETA Asia-Pacific
- Your Mommy Kills Animals (film)

Further reading

- PETA homepage [2], accessed July 2, 2010.
- McCartney, Stella. "Fur farm investigation" [3], PETAtv.com, accessed July 2, 2010.
- Morrison, A.R. Personal Reflections on the "Animal-Rights" Phenomenon [4], *The Physiologist*, Volume 44, Number 1, February 2001, accessed July 17, 2010.
- Pence, Gregory. *Classic Cases in Medical Ethics: Accounts of Cases That Have Shaped Medical Ethics* [5]. McGraw-Hill, 2007.
- PETA. Meet Your Meat [6], a film about the egg and meat industries, narrated by Alec Baldwin, accessed July 2, 2010.
- *The Huffington Post.* The Sexiest PETA Ads Of All Time! [7] a slideshow, accessed July 2, 2010.
- Workman, Dave P. *Peta Files: The Dark Side of the Animal Rights Movement* [8], Merril Press, 2003.

Animal Liberation Front

Founders	Ronnie Lee
Founded	1976
Location	Active in over 40 countries
Origins	England
Focus	Animal rights
Method	Direct action
Motto	Any act that furthers the cause of animal liberation, where all reasonable precautions are taken not to harm human or non-human life, may be claimed as an ALF action.
Website	Animalliberationfront.com [1]

The **Animal Liberation Front** (ALF) is an international, underground leaderless resistance that engages in illegal direct action in pursuit of animal liberation. Activists see themselves as a modern-day Underground Railroad, removing animals from laboratories and farms, destroying facilities, arranging safe houses and veterinary care, and operating sanctuaries where the animals live out the rest of their lives.

Active in over 40 countries, ALF cells operate clandestinely, consisting of small groups of friends and sometimes just one person, which makes the movement difficult for the authorities to monitor. Robin Webb of the British Animal Liberation Press Office has said: "That is why the ALF cannot be smashed, it cannot be effectively infiltrated, it cannot be stopped. You, each and every one of you: you are the ALF."

Activists say the movement is non-violent. According to the ALF's code, any act that furthers the cause of animal liberation, where all reasonable precautions are taken not to harm human or non-human life, may be claimed as an ALF action. American activist Rod Coronado said in 2006: "One thing that I know that separates us from the people we are constantly accused of being—that is, terrorists, violent criminals—is the fact that we have harmed no one."

There has nevertheless been widespread criticism that ALF spokespersons and activists have either failed to condemn acts of violence or have themselves engaged in it, either in the name of the ALF or under another banner. The criticism has been accompanied by dissent within the animal rights movement itself about the use of violence, and increasing attention from the police and intelligence communities. In 2002 the Southern Poverty Law Center (SPLC), which monitors extremism in the U.S., noted the involvement of the ALF in the Stop Huntingdon Animal Cruelty campaign, which SPLC identified as using terrorist tactics—though a later SPLC report also noted that while eco-radicals such as the ALF engage in property damage, they have killed no one. In 2005 the ALF was included in a United States Department of Homeland Security planning document listing a number of domestic terrorist threats on which the U.S. government expected to focus resources. In the UK, ALF actions are regarded as examples of domestic extremism, and are handled by the National Extremism Tactical Coordination Unit, set up in 2004 to monitor ALF and other illegal animal rights activity.

Origins

Band of Mercy

The roots of the ALF trace back to December 1963, when British journalist John Prestige was assigned to cover a Devon and Somerset Staghounds event, where he watched hunters chase and kill a pregnant deer. In protest, he formed the Hunt Saboteurs Association (HSA), which evolved into groups of volunteers trained to thwart the hunts' hounds by blowing horns and laying false scents.

Animal rights writer Noel Molland writes that one of these HSA groups was formed in 1971 by a law student from Luton, Ronnie Lee. In 1972, Lee and a fellow activist, Cliff Goodman, decided more militant tactics were needed. They revived the name of a 19th-century RSPCA youth group, The Bands of Mercy, and with about half a dozen activists set up the Band of Mercy, which attacked hunters' vehicles by slashing tires and breaking windows, designed to stop the hunt from even beginning, rather than thwarting it once underway.

In 1973, the Band learned that Hoechst Pharmaceuticals was building a research laboratory near Milton Keynes. On November 10, 1973, two activists set fire to the building, causing £26,000 worth of damage, returning six days later to set fire to what was left of it. It was the animal liberation movement's first known act of arson. In June 1974, two Band activists set fire to boats taking part in the annual seal cull off the Norfolk coast, which Molland writes was the last time the cull took place. Between June and August 1974, the Band launched eight raids against animal-testing laboratories, and others against chicken breeders and gun shops, damaging buildings or vehicles. Its first act of "animal liberation" took place during the same period when activists removed half a dozen guinea pigs from a guinea pig farm in Wiltshire, after which the owner closed the business, fearing further attacks. Then, as now, the use of violence against property caused a split within the fledgling movement. In July 1974, the Hunt Saboteurs Association offered a £250 reward for information leading to the identification of the Band of Mercy, telling the press, "We approve of their ideals, but are opposed to their methods."

ALF formed

In August 1974, Lee and Goodman were arrested for taking part in a raid on Oxford Laboratory Animal Colonies in Bicester, earning them the moniker the "Bicester Two." Daily demonstrations took place outside the court during their trial; Lee's local Labour MP, Ivor Clemitson, was one of their supporters. They were sentenced to three years in prison, during which Lee went on the movement's first hunger strike to obtain vegan food and clothing. They were paroled after 12 months, Lee emerging in the spring of 1976 more militant than ever. He gathered together the remaining Band of Mercy activists and two dozen new recruits, 30 in all. Molland writes that the Band of Mercy name sounded wrong as a description of what Lee saw as a revolutionary movement. Lee wanted a name that would haunt those who used animals, according to Molland. Thus, the Animal Liberation Front was born.

Structure and aims

Underground and above-ground

The movement has underground and above-ground components, and is entirely decentralized with no formal hierarchy, the absence of which acts as a firebreak when it comes to legal responsibility. Members are expected to stick to the ALF's stated aims when using its banner:

- To inflict economic damage on those who profit from the misery and exploitation of animals.
- To liberate animals from places of abuse, i.e. laboratories, factory farms, fur farms etc., and place them in good homes where they may live out their natural lives, free from suffering.
- To reveal the horror and atrocities committed against animals behind locked doors, by performing nonviolent direct actions and liberations
- To take all necessary precautions against harming any animal, human and non-human.
- Any group of people who are vegetarians or vegans and who carry out actions according to ALF guidelines have the right to regard themselves as part of the ALF.

A number of above-ground groups exist to support members of the ALF convicted of illegal actions. The Animal Liberation Front Supporters Group (ALF SG) adopts members in jail as prisoners of conscience. The Vegan Prisoners Support Group, created in 1994 when British activist Keith Mann was first jailed, works with prison authorities in the UK to ensure that ALF prisoners have access to vegan supplies. The Animal Liberation Press Office receives and publicizes anonymous communiqués from members; it operates as an ostensibly independent group funded by public donations, though the High Court in London ruled in 2006 that its press officer in the UK, Robin Webb, was a pivotal figure in the ALF.

There are three publications associated with the ALF. *Arkangel* is a British bi-annual magazine founded by Ronnie Lee. *Bite Back* is a website where members leave claims of responsibility; it published a "Direct Action Report" in 2005 stating that, in 2004 alone, ALF members had stolen 17,262 animals from facilities, and had claimed 554 acts of vandalism and arson. *No Compromise* is a San Francisco-based website that also reports on ALF actions.

Philosophy of direct action

ALF activists argue that animals should not be viewed as property, and that scientists and industry have no right to assume ownership of living beings who in the words of philosopher Tom Regan are the "subjects-of-a-life." In the view of the ALF, to fail to recognize this is an example of speciesism—the ascription of different values to beings on the basis of their species membership alone, which they argue is as ethically flawed as racism or sexism. They reject the animal welfarist position that more humane treatment is needed for animals; they say their aim is empty cages, not bigger ones. Activists argue that the animals they remove from laboratories or farms are "liberated," not "stolen," because they were never rightfully owned in the first place.

> *Labs raided, locks glued, products spiked, depots ransacked, windows smashed, construction halted, mink set free, fences torn down, cabs burnt out, offices in flames, car tires slashed, cages emptied, phone lines severed, slogans daubed, muck spread, damage done, electrics cut, site flooded, hunt dogs stolen, fur coats slashed, buildings destroyed, foxes freed, kennels attacked, businesses burgled, uproar, anger, outrage, balaclava clad thugs. It's an ALF thing!* — Keith Mann

Although the ALF rejects physical violence, many activists deny that attacks on property count as violent action, comparing the destruction of animal laboratories and other facilities to resistance fighters blowing up gas chambers in Nazi Germany. Their argument for sabotage is that the removal of animals from a laboratory simply means they will be quickly replaced, but if the laboratory itself is destroyed, it not only slows down the restocking process, but increases costs, possibly to the point of making animal research prohibitively expensive; this, they argue, will encourage the search for alternatives. An ALF activist involved in an arson attack on the University of Arizona told *No Compromise* in 1996: "[I]t is much the same thing as the abolitionists who fought against slavery going in and burning down the quarters or tearing down the auction block ... Sometimes when you just take animals and do nothing else, perhaps that is not as strong a message."

The provision against violence in the ALF code has triggered divisions within the movement and allegations of hypocrisy from the ALF's critics. In 1998, terrorism expert Paul Wilkinson said the ALF and its splinter groups were "the most serious domestic terrorist threat within the United Kingdom". In 1993, ALF was listed as an organization that has "claimed to have perpetrated acts of extremism in the United States" in the Report to Congress on the Extent and Effects of Domestic and International Terrorism on Animal Enterprises. It was named as a terrorist threat by the U.S. Department of Homeland Security in January 2005. In March 2005, a speech from the Counterterrorism Division of the FBI stated that: "The eco-terrorist movement has given rise and notoriety to groups such as the Animal Liberation Front, or ALF, and the Earth Liberation Front, or ELF. These groups exist to commit serious acts of vandalism, and to harass and intimidate owners and employees of the business sector." In hearings held on May 18, 2005 before a Senate panel, officials of the FBI and the Bureau of Alcohol, Tobacco, Firearms, and Explosives (ATF) stated that "violent animal rights extremists and eco-terrorists now pose one of the most serious terrorism threats to the nation." The use of the terrorist label has been criticized, however; the Southern Poverty Law Center, which tracks U.S. domestic extremism, writes that "for all the property damage they have wreaked, eco-radicals have killed no one."

Philosopher Steven Best and trauma surgeon Jerry Vlasak, both of whom have volunteered for the North American press office, were banned from entering the UK in 2004 and 2005 after making statements that appeared to support violence. Vlasak told an animal rights conferences in 2003: "I don't think you'd have to kill—assassinate—too many vivisectors before you would see a marked decrease in the amount of vivisection going on. And I think for five lives, 10 lives, 15 human lives, we could save a million, two million, 10 million non-human animals." Best has coined the term "extensional self-defense" to describe actions carried out in defense of animals by human beings acting as proxies. He argues that, in carrying out acts of extensional self-defense, activists have the moral right to engage in acts of sabotage or even violence, because animals are unable to fight back themselves. Best argues that the principle of extensional self defense mirrors the penal code statues known as the "necessity defense," which can be invoked when a defendant believes the illegal act was necessary to avoid imminent and great harm.

The nature of the ALF as a leaderless resistance means support for Vlasak and Best is hard to measure. An anonymous volunteer interviewed in 2005 for CBS's *60 Minutes* said of Vlasak: "[H]e doesn't operate with our endorsement or our support or our appreciation, the support of the ALF. We have a strict code of non-violence ... I don't know who put Dr. Vlasak in the position he's in. It wasn't us, the ALF."

Philosopher Peter Singer of Princeton University has argued that ALF direct action can only be regarded as a just cause if it is non-violent, and that the ALF is at its most effective when uncovering evidence of animal abuse that other tactics could not expose. He cites as an example the 1984 ALF raid on the University of Pennsylvania head-injury research clinic, during which the ALF removed footage shot by the researchers that showed them laughing at conscious baboons being brain damaged. The university responded that the treatment of the animals conformed to National Institutes of Health guidelines, but as a result of the publicity, the lab was closed down, the chief veterinarian fired, and the university placed on probation. Barbara Orlans, a former animal researcher with the NIH, now with the Kennedy Institute of Ethics, writes that the case stunned the biomedical community, and is today considered one of the most significant cases in the ethics of using animals in research. Singer argues that if the ALF would focus on this kind of direct action, instead of sabotage, it would appeal to the minds of reasonable people. Against this, Steven Best writes that industries and governments have too much institutional and financial bias for reason to prevail.

Peter Hughes of the University of Sunderland cites a 1988 raid in the UK led by ALF activist Barry Horne as an example of positive ALF direct action. Horne and four other activists decided to free Rocky, a dolphin who had lived in a small concrete pool in Marineland in Brighton for 20 years, by moving him 200 yards (180 m) from his pool to the sea. The police spotted them carrying a home-made dolphin stretcher, and they were convicted of conspiracy to steal, but they continued to campaign for Rocky's release. Marineland eventually agreed to sell him for £120,000, money that was raised with the help of the Born Free Foundation and the *Mail on Sunday*, and in 1991 Rocky was transferred to an 80-acre (320000 m^2) lagoon reserve in the Turks and Caicos Islands, then released. Hughes writes that the ALF action helped to create a paradigm shift in the UK toward seeing dolphins as "individual actors," as a result of which, he writes, there are now no captive dolphins in the UK.

Early tactics and ideology

Main article: Timeline of Animal Liberation Front actions, 1976-1999

Rachel Monaghan of the University of Ulster writes that, in their first year of operation alone, ALF actions accounted for £250,000 worth of damage, targeting butchers shops, furriers, circuses, slaughterhouses, breeders, and fast-food restaurants. She writes that the ALF philosophy was that violence can only take place against sentient life forms, and therefore focusing on property destruction and the removal of animals from laboratories and farms was consistent with a philosophy of non-violence, despite the damage they were causing. Writing in 1974, Ronnie Lee was insistent that direct action be "limited only by reverence of life and hatred of violence," and in 1979, he wrote that many ALF raids had been called off because of the risk to life.

Kim Stallwood, a national organizer for the British Union for the Abolition of Vivisection (BUAV) in the 1980s, writes that the public's response to early ALF raids that removed animals was very positive, in large measure because of the non-violence policy. When Mike Huskisson removed three beagles from a tobacco study at ICI in June 1975, the media portrayed him as a hero. Robin Webb writes that ALF volunteers were viewed as the "Robin Hoods of the animal welfare world."

This glamorization of the movement attracted a new breed of activist, Stallwood writes. They were younger, often unemployed, and more interested in anarchism than in animal liberation *per se*. Stallwood writes that they saw ALF activism as part of their opposition to the state, rather than as an end-in-itself, and did not want to adhere to non-violence. In the early 1980s, the BUAV, an anti-vivisection group founded by Frances Power Cobbe in 1898, was among the ALF's supporters. Stallwood writes that it donated part of its office space rent-free to the ALF Supporters Group, and gave ALF actions uncritical support in its newspaper, *The Liberator*. In 1982, a group of ALF activists, including Roger Yates, now a sociology lecturer at University College, Dublin, and Dave McColl, a director of Sea Shepherd, became members of the BUAV's executive committee, and used their position to radicalize the organization. Stallwood writes that the new executive believed all political action to be a waste of time,

The acronym ALF within the anarchy-A symbol.

and wanted the BUAV to devote its resources exclusively to direct action. Whereas the earliest activists had been committed to rescuing animals, and destroyed property only where it contributed to the former, by the mid-1980s, Stallwood believed the ALF had lost its ethical foundation, and had become an opportunity "for misfits and misanthropes to seek personal revenge for some perceived social injustice." He writes: "Where was the intelligent debate about tactics and strategies that went beyond the mindless rhetoric and emotional elitism pervading much of the self-produced direct action literature? In short, what had happened to the animals' interests?" In 1984, the BUAV board reluctantly voted to expel the ALF SG from its premises and withdraw its political support, after which, Stallwood writes, the ALF became increasingly isolated.

Development of the ALF in the U.S.

There are conflicting accounts of when the ALF first emerged in the United States. The FBI writes that animal rights activists had a history of committing low-level criminal activity in the U.S. dating back to the 1970s. Freeman Wicklund and Kim Stallwood say the first ALF action there was on May 29, 1977, when researchers Ken LeVasseur and Steve Sipman released two dolphins, Puka and Kea, into the ocean from the University of Hawaii's Marine Mammal Laboratory. The North American Animal Liberation Press Office attributes the dolphin release to a group called Undersea Railroad, and says the first ALF action was, in fact, a raid on the New York University Medical Center on March 14, 1979, when activists removed one cat, two dogs, and two guinea pigs.

Kathy Snow Guillermo writes in *Monkey Business* that the first ALF action was the removal on September 22, 1981 of the Silver Spring monkeys, 17 lab monkeys in the legal custody of People for the Ethical Treatment of Animals (PETA), after a researcher who had been experimenting on them was arrested for alleged violations of cruelty legislation. When the court ruled that the monkeys be returned to the researcher, they mysteriously disappeared, only to reappear five days later when PETA learned that legal action against the researcher could not proceed without the monkeys as evidence.

Ingrid Newkirk, the president of PETA, writes that the first ALF cell was set up in late 1982, after a police officer she calls "Valerie" responded to the publicity triggered by the Silver Spring monkeys case, and flew to England to be trained by the ALF. Posing as a reporter, Valerie was put in touch with Ronnie Lee by Kim Stallwood, who at the time was working for the BUAV. Lee directed her to a training camp, where she was taught how to break into laboratories. Newkirk writes that Valerie returned to Maryland and set up an ALF cell, with the first raid taking place on December 24, 1982 against Howard University, where 24 cats were removed, some of whose back legs had been crippled. Jo Shoesmith, an American attorney and animal rights activist, says Newkirk's account of "Valerie" is not only fictionalized, as Newkirk acknowledges, but totally fictitious.

Two early ALF raids led to the closure of several university studies. A raid on May 28, 1984 on the University of Pennsylvania's head injury clinic caused $60,000 worth of damage and saw the removal of 60 hours of tapes, which showed the researchers laughing as they used a hydraulic device to cause brain damage to baboons. The tapes were turned over to PETA, who produced a 26-minute video called *Unnecessary Fuss*. As a result of the publicity, the head injury clinic was closed, the university's chief veterinarian was fired, and the university was put on probation.

On April 20, 1985, acting on a tip-off from a student, the ALF raided a laboratory in the University of California, Riverside, causing nearly $700,000 worth of damage and removing 468 animals. These included Britches, a five-week old macaque monkey, who had been separated from his mother at birth and left alone with his eyes sewn shut and a sonar device on his head, as part of a study into blindness. As a result of the raid, which was taped by the ALF (video [2]), eight of the 17 research projects active at the laboratory at the time were shut down, and the university said years of medical research were lost. The raid prompted James Wyngaarden, head of the National Institutes of Health, to argue that raids on laboratories should be regarded as acts of terrorism.

Animal Rights Militia and Justice Department

Monaghan writes that, around 1982, there was a noticeable shift in the non-violent position, and not one approved by everyone in the movement. Some activists began to make personal threats against individuals, followed by letter bombs and threats to contaminate food, the latter representing yet another shift to threatening the general public, rather than specific targets.

In 1982, letter bombs were sent to all four major party leaders in England, including the prime minister, Margaret Thatcher. In November 1984, the first major food scare was carried out, with the ALF claiming in phone calls and letters to the media that it had contaminated Mars Bars—part of a campaign to force the Mars company to stop conducting tooth decay tests on monkeys. On November 17, the *Sunday Mirror* received a call from the ALF saying it had injected Mars Bars in stores throughout the country with rat poison. The call was followed by a letter containing a Mars Bar, presumed to be contaminated, and the claim that these were on sale in London, Leeds, York, Southampton, and Coventry. Millions of bars were removed from shelves and Mars halted production, at a cost to the company of $4.5 million. The ALF admitted the claims had been a hoax. Similar contamination claims were later made against L'Oréal and Lucozade.

The letter bombs were claimed by the Animal Rights Militia (ARM), although the initial statement in November 1984 by David Mellor, then a Home Office minister, made clear that it was the Animal Liberation Front who had claimed responsibility. This is an early example of the shifting of responsibility from one banner to another depending on the nature of the act, with the ARM and another *nom de guerre*, the Justice Department—the latter first used in 1993—emerging as names for direct action that violated the ALF's "no harm to living beings" principle. Ronnie Lee, who had earlier insisted on the importance of the ALF's non-violence policy, seemed to support the idea. An article signed by RL—presumed to be Ronnie Lee—in the October 1984 ALF Supporters Group newsletter, suggested that activists set up "fresh groups ... under new names whose policies do not preclude the use of violence toward animal abusers."

No activist is known to have conducted operations under both the ALF and ARM banners, but the overlap is assumed. Terrorism expert Paul Wilkinson has written that the ALF, the Justice Department, and the ARM are essentially the same thing, and Robert Garner of the University of Leicester writes that it would be pointless to argue otherwise, given the nature of the movement as a leaderless resistance. Robin Webb of the British Animal Liberation Press Office has acknowledged that the activists may be the same people: "If someone wishes to act as the Animal Rights Militia or the Justice Department, simply put, the ... policy of the Animal Liberation Front, to take all reasonable precautions not to endanger life, no longer applies."

From 1983 onwards, a series of fire bombs exploded in department stores that sold fur, with the intention of triggering the sprinkler systems in order to cause damage, although several stores were partly or completely destroyed. In September 1985, incendiary devices were placed under the cars of Dr. Sharat Gangoli and Dr. Stuart Walker, both animal researchers with the British Industrial Biological Research Association (BIBRA), wrecking both vehicles but with no injuries, and with the ARM claiming responsibility. In January 1986, the ARM said it had placed devices under the cars of four employees of Huntingdon Life Sciences, timed to explode an hour apart from each other. A further device was placed under the car of Dr. Andor Sebesteny, a researcher for the Imperial Cancer Research Fund, which he spotted before it exploded.

False flags and plausible deniability

The nature of the ALF exposes its name to the risk of being used by activists who reject its non-violence platform, or by opponents conducting so-called "false-flag" operations, designed to make the ALF appear violent. That same uncertainty provides genuine ALF activists with plausible deniability should an operation go wrong, by denying that the act was "authentically ALF".

Several incidents in 1989 and 1990 were described by the movement as false flag operations. In February 1989, an explosion damaged the Senate House bar in Bristol University, an attack claimed by the unknown "Animal Abused Society". In June 1990, two days apart, bombs exploded in the cars of Margaret Baskerville, a veterinary surgeon working at Porton Down, a chemical research defence establishment, and Patrick Max Headley, a psychologist at Bristol University. Baskerville escaped without injury by jumping through the window of her mini-jeep when a bomb using a mercury-tilt device exploded next to the fuel tank. During the attack on Headley, which *New Scientist* writes involved the use of plastic explosives, a 13-month-old baby passing by in a stroller suffered flash burns, shrapnel wounds to his back, and a partially severed finger.

No known entity claimed responsibility for the attacks, which were condemned within the animal rights movement and by ALF activists. Keith Mann writes that it did not seem plausible that activists known for making simple incendiary devices from household components would suddenly switch to mercury-tilt switches and plastic explosives, then never be heard from again. A few days after the bombings, the unknown "British Animal Rights Society" claimed responsibility for having attached a nail bomb to a huntsman's Land Rover in Somerset. Forensic evidence led police to arrest the owner of the vehicle, who admitted he had bombed his own car to discredit the animal rights movement, and asked for two similar offences to be taken into consideration. He was jailed for nine months. The Baskerville and Headley bombers were never apprehended.

1996 onwards

Further information: Consort beagles, Save the Hillgrove Cats, Stop Huntingdon Animal Cruelty, Save the Newchurch Guinea Pigs, SPEAK campaign, Timeline of Animal Liberation Front actions, 2000-2004, and Timeline of Animal Liberation Front actions, 2005-Present

Violence against property began to increase substantially after several high-profile campaigns closed down facilities perceived to be abusive to animals. Consort Kennels, a facility breeding beagles for animal testing; Hillgrove Farm, which bred cats; and Newchurch Farm, which bred guinea pigs, were all closed after being targeted by animal rights campaigns that appeared to involve the ALF. In the UK, the financial year 1991–1992 saw around 100 refrigerated meat trucks destroyed by incendiary devices at a cost of around £5 million. Butchers' locks were superglued, shrink-wrapped meats were pierced in supermarkets, slaughterhouses and refrigerated meat trucks were set on fire.

In 1999, ALF activists became involved in the international Stop Huntingdon Animal Cruelty (SHAC) campaign to close Huntingdon Life Sciences (HLS), Europe's largest animal-testing laboratory. The Southern Poverty Law Center, which monitors U.S. domestic extremism, has described SHAC's *modus operandi* as "frankly terroristic tactics similar to those of anti-abortion extremists." ALF activist Donald Currie was jailed for 12 years and placed on probation for life in December 2006 after being found guilty of planting homemade bombs on the doorsteps of businessmen with links to HLS. HLS director Brian Cass was attacked by men wielding pick-axe handles in February 2001, an attack so serious that Detective Chief Inspector Tom Hobbs of Cambridgeshire police said it was only by sheer luck that they were not starting a murder inquiry. David Blenkinsop was one of those convicted of the attack, someone who in the past had conducted actions in the name of the ALF.

Also in 1999, a freelance reporter, Graham Hall, said he had been attacked after producing a documentary critical of the ALF, which was aired on Channel 4. The documentary showed ALF press officer, Robin Webb, appearing to give Hall—who was filming undercover and purporting to be an activist—advice about how to make an improvised explosive device, though Webb said his comments had been used out of context. Hall said that, as a result of the documentary, he was abducted, tied to a chair, and had the letters "ALF" branded on his back, before being released 12 hours later with a warning not to tell the police.

In June 2006, the ALF claimed responsibility for a firebomb attack on University of California, Los Angeles researcher Lynn Fairbanks, after a firebomb was placed on the doorstep of a house occupied by her 70 year-old tenant; according to the FBI, it was powerful enough to have killed the occupants, but failed to ignite. The attack was credited by the acting chancellor of UCLA as helping to shape the

Animal Enterprise Terrorism Act. Animal liberation press officer Jerry Vlasak said of the attack: "force is a poor second choice, but if that's the only thing that will work ... there's certainly moral justification for that." As of 2008, activists were increasingly taking protests to the homes of researchers, staging "home demonstrations," which can involve making noise during the night, writing slogans on the researchers' property, smashing windows, and spreading rumours to neighbours.

Operation Backfire

Further information: Earth Liberation Front#Cooperation with the ALF

On January 20, 2006, as part of *Operation Backfire*, the U.S. Department of Justice announced charges against nine American and two Canadian activists calling themselves the "family," who are alleged to have engaged in direct action in the name of the ALF and ELF. The Department of Justice called the acts examples of "domestic terrorism." Environmental and animal rights activists have referred to the legal action as the *Green Scare*. The incidents included arson attacks against meat-processing plants, lumber companies, a high-tension power line, and a ski center, in Oregon, Wyoming, Washington, California, and Colorado between 1996 and 2001.

See also

- Deep ecology
- GANDALF trial
- Green anarchism

Further reading

- Animal Liberation Front [3], accessed June 6, 2010.
- ALF North American Press Office FAQ [4], accessed June 6, 2010.
- "Terrorism 2000 / 2001" [5], FBI document mentioning the ALF, accessed June 6, 2010.
- Tester, Keith. "The British experience of the militant opposition to the agricultural use of animals" [6], *Journal of Agricultural and Environmental Ethics*, Volume 2, Number 3, September 1989.
- Young, Peter Daniel (2010). *Animal Liberation Front: Complete Diary of Actions, The First 30 Years'*. *Voice of the Voiceless Communications* [7]. ISBN 9780984284405

Article Sources and Contributors

Abandoned pets *Source*: http://en.wikipedia.org/?oldid=384523435 *Contributors*: Hearfourmewesique

Animal hoarding *Source*: http://en.wikipedia.org/?oldid=388383370 *Contributors*: Gfoley4

Cruelty to animals *Source*: http://en.wikipedia.org/?oldid=390417140 *Contributors*: Materialscientist

Animal testing *Source*: http://en.wikipedia.org/?oldid=390255005 *Contributors*: Yerpo

History of animal testing *Source*: http://en.wikipedia.org/?oldid=390462233 *Contributors*: Bongwarrior

Animal law *Source*: http://en.wikipedia.org/?oldid=385760274 *Contributors*: Wikignome0530

Animal rights *Source*: http://en.wikipedia.org/?oldid=390513648 *Contributors*: Bilby

Speciesism *Source*: http://en.wikipedia.org/?oldid=389756819 *Contributors*: 1 anonymous edits

Animal welfare *Source*: http://en.wikipedia.org/?oldid=390352124 *Contributors*: Tryptofish

Intrinsic value (animal ethics) *Source*: http://en.wikipedia.org/?oldid=385816038 *Contributors*: Wikignome0530

Abolitionism (animal rights) *Source*: http://en.wikipedia.org/?oldid=371879758 *Contributors*: Tryptofish

Wildlife management *Source*: http://en.wikipedia.org/?oldid=390525351 *Contributors*: Look2See1

Veganarchism *Source*: http://en.wikipedia.org/?oldid=386512780 *Contributors*: Rich Farmbrough

Animal liberation movement *Source*: http://en.wikipedia.org/?oldid=379537928 *Contributors*: Gobonobo

People for the Ethical Treatment of Animals *Source*: http://en.wikipedia.org/?oldid=389956773 *Contributors*: WikHead

Animal Liberation Front *Source*: http://en.wikipedia.org/?oldid=388665309 *Contributors*:

Image Sources, Licenses and Contributors

File:Q 005717HoreseInGasMaskPilckemRidge31October1917.jpg *Source*: http://bibliocm.bibliolabs.com/mwAnon/index.php?title=File:Q_005717HoreseInGasMaskPilckemRidge31October1917.jpg *License*: unknown *Contributors*: Photographer: Brooke J W (Lt)

File:NASAchimp.jpg *Source*: http://bibliocm.bibliolabs.com/mwAnon/index.php?title=File:NASAchimp.jpg *License*: unknown *Contributors*: -

Image:An Experiment on a Bird in an Air Pump by Joseph Wright of Derby, 1768.jpg *Source*: http://bibliocm.bibliolabs.com/mwAnon/index.php?title=File:An_Experiment_on_a_Bird_in_an_Air_Pump_by_Joseph_Wright_of_Derby,_1768.jpg *License*: unknown *Contributors*: -

Image:Claude Bernard 5.jpg *Source*: http://bibliocm.bibliolabs.com/mwAnon/index.php?title=File:Claude_Bernard_5.jpg *License*: unknown *Contributors*: -

Image:One of Pavlov's dogs.jpg *Source*: http://bibliocm.bibliolabs.com/mwAnon/index.php?title=File:One_of_Pavlov's_dogs.jpg *License*: GNU Free Documentation License *Contributors*: Rklawton

File:Types of vertebrates v2en.png *Source*: http://bibliocm.bibliolabs.com/mwAnon/index.php?title=File:Types_of_vertebrates_v2en.png *License*: unknown *Contributors*: -

Image:Drosophila melanogaster - front (aka).jpg *Source*: http://bibliocm.bibliolabs.com/mwAnon/index.php?title=File:Drosophila_melanogaster_-_front_(aka).jpg *License*: Creative Commons Attribution-Sharealike 2.5 *Contributors*: user:Aka

Image:Wistar rat.jpg *Source*: http://bibliocm.bibliolabs.com/mwAnon/index.php?title=File:Wistar_rat.jpg *License*: unknown *Contributors*: -

File:Frog vivisection.jpg *Source*: http://bibliocm.bibliolabs.com/mwAnon/index.php?title=File:Frog_vivisection.jpg *License*: unknown *Contributors*: -

Image:DraizeTest-PETA.jpg *Source*: http://bibliocm.bibliolabs.com/mwAnon/index.php?title=File:DraizeTest-PETA.jpg *License*: Public Domain *Contributors*: Gobonobo, Nard the Bard, SlimVirgin, 1 anonymous edits

Image:Dollyscotland (crop).jpg *Source*: http://bibliocm.bibliolabs.com/mwAnon/index.php?title=File:Dollyscotland_(crop).jpg *License*: unknown *Contributors*: -

Image:Veterinary Surgeon.jpg *Source*: http://bibliocm.bibliolabs.com/mwAnon/index.php?title=File:Veterinary_Surgeon.jpg *License*: unknown *Contributors*: Abujoy, AndreasPraefcke, Ed g2s, Solipsist, Tano4595, Una Smith, Uwe Gille, Wst, 1 anonymous edits

Image:Olive baboon1.jpg *Source*: http://bibliocm.bibliolabs.com/mwAnon/index.php?title=File:Olive_baboon1.jpg *License*: unknown *Contributors*: -

Image:God2-Sistine Chapel.png *Source*: http://bibliocm.bibliolabs.com/mwAnon/index.php?title=File:God2-Sistine_Chapel.png *License*: unknown *Contributors*: User:QuartierLatin1968

Image:Jean-Jacques Rousseau (painted portrait).jpg *Source*: http://bibliocm.bibliolabs.com/mwAnon/index.php?title=File:Jean-Jacques_Rousseau_(painted_portrait).jpg *License*: unknown *Contributors*: -

Image:Jeremy Bentham by Henry William Pickersgill detail.jpg *Source*: http://bibliocm.bibliolabs.com/mwAnon/index.php?title=File:Jeremy_Bentham_by_Henry_William_Pickersgill_detail.jpg *License*: Public Domain *Contributors*: Henry William Pickersgill (died 1875)

Image:Smithfield Last day of Old Smithfield ILN 1855.jpg *Source*: http://bibliocm.bibliolabs.com/mwAnon/index.php?title=File:Smithfield_Last_day_of_Old_Smithfield_ILN_1855.jpg *License*: unknown *Contributors*: -

Image:Badger-baiting3.jpg *Source*: http://bibliocm.bibliolabs.com/mwAnon/index.php?title=File:Badger-baiting3.jpg *License*: Public Domain *Contributors*: User:Kelly

Image:Trial of Bill Burns.jpg *Source*: http://bibliocm.bibliolabs.com/mwAnon/index.php?title=File:Trial_of_Bill_Burns.jpg *License*: Public Domain *Contributors*: Original uploader was SlimVirgin at en.wikipedia

Image:Arthur Schopenhauer Portrait by Ludwig Sigismund Ruhl 1815.jpeg *Source*: http://bibliocm.bibliolabs.com/mwAnon/index.php?title=File:Arthur_Schopenhauer_Portrait_by_Ludwig_Sigismund_Ruhl_1815.jpeg *License*: unknown *Contributors*: -

Image:Highgaterabbit.jpg *Source*: http://bibliocm.bibliolabs.com/mwAnon/index.php?title=File:Highgaterabbit.jpg *License*: unknown *Contributors*: -

Image:Prof. Dr. Carl Cohen (cropped).jpg *Source*: http://bibliocm.bibliolabs.com/mwAnon/index.php?title=File:Prof._Dr._Carl_Cohen_(cropped).jpg *License*: Creative Commons Attribution-Sharealike 2.0 *Contributors*: Rainer Ebert

File:Trial of Bill Burns.jpg *Source*: http://bibliocm.bibliolabs.com/mwAnon/index.php?title=File:Trial_of_Bill_Burns.jpg *License*: Public Domain *Contributors*: Original uploader was SlimVirgin at en.wikipedia

File:FEMA - 3634 - Photograph by Leif Skoogfors taken on 07-21-2001 in West Virginia.jpg *Source*: http://bibliocm.bibliolabs.com/mwAnon/index.php?title=File:FEMA_-_3634_-_Photograph_by_Leif_Skoogfors_taken_on_07-21-2001_in_West_Virginia.jpg *License*: Public Domain *Contributors*: Martin H.

Image:White-tailed deer.jpg *Source*: http://bibliocm.bibliolabs.com/mwAnon/index.php?title=File:White-tailed_deer.jpg *License*: Public Domain *Contributors*: User:NuclearWarfare

File:Veganarchism.svg *Source*: http://bibliocm.bibliolabs.com/mwAnon/index.php?title=File:Veganarchism.svg *License*: unknown *Contributors*: User:Froztbyte

File:Anarchy-symbol.svg *Source*: http://bibliocm.bibliolabs.com/mwAnon/index.php?title=File:Anarchy-symbol.svg *License*: unknown *Contributors*: -

File:BlackFlagSymbol.svg *Source*: http://bibliocm.bibliolabs.com/mwAnon/index.php?title=File:BlackFlagSymbol.svg *License*: unknown *Contributors*: -

Image:ALF logo.svg *Source*: http://bibliocm.bibliolabs.com/mwAnon/index.php?title=File:ALF_logo.svg *License*: unknown *Contributors*: -

Image:Peter Singer.jpg *Source*: http://bibliocm.bibliolabs.com/mwAnon/index.php?title=File:Peter_Singer.jpg *License*: unknown *Contributors*: -

Image:Longbridges Fire.jpg *Source*: http://bibliocm.bibliolabs.com/mwAnon/index.php?title=File:Longbridges_Fire.jpg *License*: Public Domain *Contributors*: Original uploader was Matt86C at en.wikipedia

File:Peta Comic Book.gif *Source*: http://bibliocm.bibliolabs.com/mwAnon/index.php?title=File:Peta_Comic_Book.gif *License*: Creative Commons Attribution-Sharealike 3.0 *Contributors*: People for the Ethical Treatment of Animals (PETA)

The cover image herein is used under a Creative Commons License and may be reused or reproduced under that same license.

http://images.cdn.fotopedia.com/flickr-3652037059-hd.jpg

CPSIA information can be obtained at www.ICGtesting.com
Printed in the USA
LVOW050523141111

254838LV00004B/20/P

9 781241 719685